▶ **African-American Males and the U.S. Justice System of Marginalization**

DOI: 10.1057/9781137408433.0001

Other Palgrave Pivot titles

DOI: 10.1057/9781137408433.0001

palgrave▶pivot

African-American Males and the U.S. Justice System of Marginalization: A National Tragedy

Floyd Weatherspoon

Associate Dean for Dispute Resolution Programs and Professor of Law, Capital University Law School, USA

palgrave
macmillan

DOI: 10.1057/9781137408433.0001

AFRICAN-AMERICAN MALES AND THE U.S. JUSTICE SYSTEM OF MARGINALIZATION
Copyright © Floyd Weatherspoon, 2014.

First published in 2014 by
PALGRAVE MACMILLAN®
in the United States—a division of St. Martin's Press LLC,
175 Fifth Avenue, New York, NY 10010.

Where this book is distributed in the UK, Europe and the rest of the world,
this is by Palgrave Macmillan, a division of Macmillan Publishers Limited,
registered in England, company number 785998, of Houndmills, Basingstoke,
Hampshire RG21 6XS.

Palgrave Macmillan is the global academic imprint of the above companies
and has companies and representatives throughout the world.

Palgrave® and Macmillan® are registered trademarks in the United States,
the United Kingdom, Europe and other countries.

ISBN: 978-1-137-40845-7 EPUB
ISBN: 978-1-137-40843-3 PDF
ISBN: 978-1-137-41166-2 Hardback

Library of Congress Cataloging-in-Publication Data

Weatherspoon, Floyd D., 1951–
    African-American males and the U.S. justice system of marginalization : a
national tragedy / Floyd Weatherspoon.
        pages cm
    ISBN 978-1-137-41166-2 (hardback)
    1. Discrimination in criminal justice administration—United States.
    2. African American men—Social conditions. 3. African American men—
Economic conditions. 4. African American criminals—Civil rights. 5. Race
discrimination—United States. 6. United States—Race relations. I. Title.

HV9950.W4185 2014
364.3′7308996073—dc23   2014028132

A catalogue record of the book is available from the British Library.

First edition: 2014

www.palgrave.com/pivot

DOI: 10.1057/9781137408433

To my grandmother, Mable Short, who with a fourth grade education understood the urgency of educating black boys and rejected any notion that I could not be successful. My wife, Stephanie-Jones-Weatherspoon, has for more than 30 years supported and encouraged me to write about the plight of African-American males

DOI: 10.1057/9781137408433.0001

Contents

DOI: 10.1057/9781137408433.0001

Acknowledgments

The following law reviews have given permission to include segments of my previous publications in this book:

Capital University Law Review
Floyd D. Weatherspoon, *The Devastating Impact of The Justice System on the Status of African-American Males: An Overview Perspective*, Volume 23, Number 1 (1994).

North Carolina Central Law Review
Floyd D. Weatherspoon, *Racial Justice and Equity for African-American Males in the American Educational System: A Dream Forever Deferred*, Volume 29, Number 1 (2006).

Texas A&M Law Review
Floyd D. Weatherspoon, *The Mass Incarceration of African-American Males: A Return to Institutionalized Slavery, Oppression, and Disenfranchisement of Constitutional Rights*, Volume 13, Number 2 (2007).

John Marshall Law Review
Floyd D. Weatherspoon, *Racial Profiling of African-American Males: Stopped, Searched, and Stripped of Constitutional Protection*, Volume 38, Number 2 (Winter 2004).

University of Pittsburgh Law Review
Floyd D. Weatherspoon, *Ending Racial Profiling of African-Americans in the Selective Enforcement of Laws: In Search of Viable Remedies*, Volume 65, Issue 4 (Summer 2004).

Washburn Law Review
Floyd D. Weatherspoon, *Remedying Employment Discrimination Against African-American Males: Stereotypical Biases Engender a Case of Race Plus Sex Discrimination*, Volume 36 (Fall 1996).

Special Thanks

I would like to thank the following organizations whose research, statistics, and studies on the status of African-American males were invaluable for the completion of this book:

The Sentencing Project
U.S. Census Bureau
The Pew Research Center
The National Center for Education Statistics
The Schott Foundation for Public Education
U.S. Department of Justice, Office of Justice Programs, Bureau of Justice
    Statistics
U.S. Department of Education, National Center for Education Statistics
U.S. Department of Education, Office of Civil Rights

Personal Acknowledgments

I am especially grateful to the following Research Assistants who have worked with me on this book as well as other projects which focused on the plight of African-American males and the impact of the justice system: Rasheda Hansard, Jennifer Dick, Joshua Farnsworth, Michelle Lanham, Gregory Pace, Marley Raymond, Brandi Scales, Kathleen Smith, Jeffrey Carlino, and Sean Walton, Jr. I am also very appreciative of the following Faculty Assistants who worked patiently typing and retyping the many drafts of this book: Amy Ooten and Soni Shoemaker.

DOI: 10.1057/9781137408433.0002

Introduction

Abstract: *This introductory chapter provides an overview of the economic and social status of African-American males in America which continues to deteriorate at an alarming rate. In every American institutional system, from birth to death, the journey of African-American males to achieve racial justice and equity in this country is ignored, marginalized, and exploited. The American justice system, in particular, has permitted, and in some cases sanctioned, the marginalization of African-American males as full citizens. This chapter outlines how African-American males are disproportionately represented in every aspect of the criminal justice system: from being racially profiled, stopped, arrested, prosecuted, sentenced, and incarcerated, to even being placed on death row.*

Weatherspoon, Floyd. *African-American Males and the U.S. Justice System of Marginalization: A National Tragedy*. New York: Palgrave Macmillan, 2014. DOI: 10.1057/9781137408433.0003.

The marginalization of African-American males in America as full citizens has a long and treacherous history that continues to negatively impact their economic, political, and social status. The economic and social status of African-American males in America continues to deteriorate at an alarming rate. In every American institutional system, from birth to death, the journey of African-American males to achieve racial justice and equity in this country is ignored, marginalized, and exploited. The American justice system, in particular, has permitted, and in some cases sanctioned, the marginalization of African-American males as full citizens. The basis for the denial of racial justice and equity for African-American males is caused, in part, by the intersection of their race and gender (black and male). A combination of their immutable traits of being black and male places the burden of racial injustice on them, which most will carry for life, as it is difficult to overcome.

Similar to the mass number of Africans enslaved in America during the colonial period and prior to the Civil War, mass numbers of African-American males have temporarily or permanently lost the right to vote, the ability to freely travel without harassment from law enforcement, and the opportunity to obtain a quality public education and meaningful employment. The present-day plight of African-American males parallels the experiences of Africans who were enslaved in America and the experiences of African-Americans after Reconstruction.

African-American males are adversely and disproportionately impacted by the American justice system. The justice system is having a devastating effect on every aspect of their lives. African-American males are disproportionately represented in every aspect of the criminal justice system, from being racially profiled, stopped, arrested, prosecuted, sentenced, and incarcerated, to even being disproportionately placed on death row. African-American males are penalized without conscience, remorse, or constitutional protection. Indeed, the overrepresentation of African-American males in the criminal justice system negatively impacts their ability to gain employment, health care, credit, federal student loans, and the power to vote. In addition, African-American males are generally punished more severely than whites who commit the same or similar crimes. At the root of many of these issues is a discriminatory criminal justice system which intentionally targets African-American males for punishment and incarceration.

When African-American males seek legal redress to vindicate their legal rights within the criminal justice system, they face unyielding

DOI: 10.1057/9781137408433.0003

obstacles of bias in pursuing such claims. On any typical day in criminal court, African-American males are herded into court without adequate representation and are pressured to plea to lesser charges that result in a prison sentence and a subsequent felony record. For example, in 2007, the Jena Six' incident involving six young African-American males brought to the public's attention, again, how our justice system can be unjust when young African-American males are confronted with charges of criminal activities.

In addition to the criminal justice system, African-American males are also negatively impacted by every other American institutional system. Indeed, the public educational system has failed to meet the educational needs of African-American males. Unfortunately, the American educational system serves as a feeder for prisons and jails. In other words, public school systems provide an unlimited supply of African-American males to the criminal justice system for incarceration and a life of bondage. Our public school system can fairly be described as the twin sister to the criminal justice system, as they both house mass numbers of African-American males whose dreams are forever trammeled.

Our systems for obtaining employment, health care, financial credit, housing, and voting all negatively impact African-American males. There is no American institutional system where African-American males can escape prejudices and biases, even including the military, sports, and the media.

Statistical data unequivocally support the fact that the criminal justice system and other institutional systems negatively impact the status of African-American males. The data, however, have been cited so frequently that it is no longer shocking to our society. This readily available information has been dehumanized and trivialized to the point that it is considered just a fact of life in urban America. Some researchers have characterized African-American males as being "obsolete and dangerous," an "endangered species," and having "broken lives." The most frequently cited data on African-American males includes:

▸ African-American males in their twenties are disproportionately in jail, on probation, or on parole.
▸ African-American males are disproportionately arrested for drug violations.
▸ African-American males are disproportionately on death row.

DOI: 10.1057/9781137408433.0003

▶ African-American males are more likely to be under the supervision of corrections than enrolled in college.
▶ On any given day, African-American males are more likely to be in prison than white males.
▶ African-American males are more likely than any other group to be a victim of a homicide.

On a number of occasions, the U.S. Sentencing Commission has reported to Congress that the Federal Sentencing Guidelines unfairly and disproportionately impacted African-Americans. Nevertheless, Congress ignored the Commission's recommendations to address these glaring discrepancies for more than two decades, thus allowing mass numbers of African-American males to be incarcerated. Only recently has Congress taken meaningful steps to address the disparities in sentencing and blatant discrimination in the criminal justice system.

The recent release of innocent African-American men from prison and death row after DNA tests revealed their innocence illustrates how our criminal justice system has cracks which continue to engulf innocent African-American males into a life of imprisonment, or even death.

The devastating impact of the justice system on the status of African-American males also directly and indirectly affects other institutional systems and processes. African-American males typically rank at the bottom of every study or statistical report regarding education, health, and employment. For example:

▶ African-American males have a lower life expectancy than all other groups.
▶ African-American males are disproportionately suspended and expelled from school.
▶ African-American males have the highest dropout rate in elementary and secondary school, as well as in college (if they go at all).
▶ African-American males have one of the highest rates of unemployment.

Even though it is quite evident that there is a correlation between the plight of African-American males and their treatment by our justice system, there has been very little legal discourse, scholarship, or any concerted response from the legal community to address these issues. Various state and local organizations, legislatures, and the federal government, however, have only recently made a concerted effort to

DOI: 10.1057/9781137408433.0003

examine the deplorable status of African-American males. However, these programs are often underfunded or otherwise not effective in addressing the plight of African-American males. Statistical data on the economic and social status of African-American males continue to be collected, complied, and analyzed, which finds that they still lag behind other groups in realizing the American dream of prosperity. There has not been a comprehensive plan to address the underlying systemic patterns of isolation and exclusion from the general society that they face. Only recently has President Obama announced a federal initiative called "My Brother's Keeper" to address the many challenges African-American and Hispanic males face.[2] Clearly, the federal government cannot resolve all the entrenched challenges African-American males face. However, the federal government can take an active leadership role to encourage local and state educational and penal systems, fair employment agencies, election commissions, and the courts to develop and implement meaningful programs to address the plight of African-American males.

The beating of Rodney King by Los Angeles police in 1991 forced most Americans to admit that the law enforcement community treats African-American males differently. Nevertheless, this level of awareness has long since evaporated from the minds of most white Americans. Most Americans have never heard of, nor remember, the Malice Green incident. But for African-Americans, especially black males, the realities of the Rodney King, Malice Green, Amadou Diallo, and James Byrd incidents are a part of the fabric of their lives to be reckoned with on a daily basis.

Years later, these horrific beating of African-American males continues, a new generation of young African-American males have become victims of similar atrophies of injustices. The shooting of Trayvon Martin, an unarmed 17-year-old youth, confirmed that stereotypical biases still exist. The view that young African-American males are dangerous and to be feared, especially if they are wearing a hoodie, is the prevailing view of the public. The shooting of an unarmed man, Jonathan Ferrell, 10 times by Charlotte police, when he was seeking assistance after a serious car accident, further illustrates the peril African-Americans face on a daily basis.

The evidence is overwhelming that in America, African-American males still remain invisible, devalued, and face insidious discrimination and isolation from the mainstreams of society. Yet, there is still no

DOI: 10.1057/9781137408433.0003

comprehensive plan at any level of government, or within the African-American communities, to address these issues.

At the 2013 Commencement program at Morehouse College, President Obama stated:

> For black men in the '40s and the '50s, the threat of violence, the constant humiliations, large and small, the uncertainty that you could support a family, the gnawing doubts born of the Jim Crow culture that told you every day that somehow you were inferior, the temptation to shrink from the world, to accept your place, to avoid risks, to be afraid—that temptation was necessarily strong.[3]

Unfortunately, what President Obama described still exist for African-American males in this country. Because the evidence of insidious discrimination is so overwhelming, the logical conclusion is simple: either America is just indifferent to the plight of African-American males or is hostile to their mere existence. Either way, it is evident that a national blueprint for rebuilding, reshaping, and reestablishing the status of African-American males is urgently needed to avert a national tragedy.

The purpose of this book is to provide an overview of the plight of African-American males in this country, and to identify how their status is directly and indirectly impacted by our justice system and every other major institutional system (e.g., education, voting, and employment). In addition, the book explains why the status of African-American males in this country should be considered a national tragedy. The real tragedy is that year after year, statistical data on African-American males are collected and analyzed. The data confirm what everyone already knows: that the status of African-American males is deplorable, yet the status of African-American males continues to worsen. This book will not attempt to provide a comprehensive analysis of all the identified legal, social, and economic issues which impact African-American males, nor does it provide an exhaustive list of remedies. In this regard, it is hoped that this book will engender not only further research, scholarship, and discussion into possible remedies, but also the implementation of concrete and measureable actions from all the stakeholders.

The first part of the book identifies stereotypical biases that exist concerning African-American males and provides examples of how our justice system sanctions, perpetuates, and in some cases creates these stereotypes. The second part of the book focuses on the impact

DOI: 10.1057/9781137408433.0003

of the criminal justice system on the plight of African-American males. Finally, areas where African-American males are treated less favorably or disproportionately by other institutional systems are identified and examined.

Notes

1   *See generally*, Andrew E. Taslitz and Carol Stelker, *Introduction to the Symposium: The Jena Six, the Prosecutorial Conscience, and the Dead Hand of History*, 44 *Harv. C.R. C. L. L. Rev.* 275 (2009); *Anthony v. Alfieri, Essay: Prosecuting the Jena Six*, 93 *Cornell L. Rev.* 1285 (2008).

2   The White House, Office of the Press Secretary, Presidential Memorandum-Creating and Expanding Ladders of Opportunity for Boys and Young Men of Color, February 29, 2014, *available at* http://www.whitehouse.gov/the-press-office/2014/02/27; also see, The White House, Office of the Press Secretary, Executive Order—White House Initiative on Educational Excellence for African Americans, July 12, 2012, *available at* www.whitehouse.gov/the-press-office/2012/07/26/executive-order.

3   The White House, Office of the Press Secretary, May 19, 2013, Remarks by the President at Morehouse College Commencement Ceremony, *available at* www.whitehouse.gov/the-press-office/2013.

DOI: 10.1057/9781137408433.0003

1
Stereotypical Biases Against African-American Males

Abstract: *This chapter points out that there has been a long and treacherous history of negative stereotypical biases and attitudes about and directed at African-American males. These biases and myths toward African-American males have evolved and lingered on into the twenty-first century. African-American males as a group are often viewed by the public as having a propensity to be lazy, hostile, unintelligent, unwilling to work, refuse to take care of their families, to only strive to become a professional basketball or football player, and to engage in criminal activity. This chapter explains how their mere swagger, dress, walk and speech of African-American males are often viewed in a negative light.*

Weatherspoon, Floyd. *African-American Males and the U.S. Justice System of Marginalization: A National Tragedy.* New York: Palgrave Macmillan, 2014.
DOI: 10.1057/9781137408433.0004.

African-American males as a group are often viewed by whites and even immigrants as having a propensity to be lazy, hostile, unintelligent, irresponsible, and unwilling to work or take care of their family. They believe that African-American males only strive to become professional basketball or football players, and engage in criminal activity. Yet, images of a select few African-American males such as Bill Cosby, Colin Powell, Will Smith, and President Barack Obama are viewed as hard-working, family oriented, and patriotic. Only African-American males who project what white Americans view as the norm are viewed in a positive manner. In other words, those that have assimilated into the middle class are seen as nonthreatening black men.

There has been a long and painful history of negative stereotypical biases and attitudes about, and directed at African-American males. These stereotypical biases have existed since Africans were first brought to America as slaves. These biases and myths toward and about African-American males have since evolved and lingered on into the twenty-first century. Slavery in America ended almost 150 years ago, but negative images of African-American males by white Americans have only marginally improved; some would even suggest that they have, in fact, deteriorated, especially during the past 60 years.

Among the many stereotypical biases regarding African-American males is that they have a propensity to be violent. In part, white Americans' fears derive from the institution of slavery. Slave owners were fearful that slaves would rise up and violently retaliate against white slave owners. Today, many white Americans have no recollection or historical perspective of the Nat Turner uprising, except there is a general stereotype that African-American males react violently when confronted with conflict, especially involving white males; thus, the defense is to avoid all contacts, except sports, if possible, with African-American males. In 1950, a leaflet was distributed in a Chicago suburb which stated, among other things, that "[i]f persuasion and the need to prevent the white race from becoming marginalized by the negro will not unite us, then the aggressions...rapes, robberies, knives, guns and marijuana of the negro, surely will."[1]

More than 60 years later, these same stereotypical biases still exist. During the past century, however, one noticeable superficial metamorphosis has been obvious: what we call African-American males. African-American males have gone from being called a "Mandingo" during slavery, to "nigger boy" in the 1930s and the 1940s, to "nigga" or

DOI: 10.1057/9781137408433.0004

"negro" in the 1950s and the 1960s, to "black" male in the 1970s and the 1980s, to the present politically correct term, "African-American" male. However, most recently, the term "thug" has been used to describe an African-American male, which is considered another derogatory and racist name.[2] During each of these periods, stereotypical biases about African-American males can be identified. They include having sexual prowess, ignorance, lack of skill and education, violent tendencies, and arrogance. Unfortunately, these negative perceptions and fears of African-American males by white Americans during these periods did not end as a decade ended, but carried forward to become permanently ingrained in our American culture.

White Americans, as well as other minority groups, are steeped with such negative stereotypical attitudes and images about African-American males that most major institutional and organizational systems adversely impact African-American males. Whether it is the country's educational system, the judicial system (both civil and criminal), the military, the media, housing, health, politics, or even sports, African-American males are negatively perceived and disproportionately impacted by policies and practices.

It is interesting to note that in the area of sports, African-American males are loved and admired by white fans. Often the ability to play sports transcends the issue of race while engaged in playing sports. However, African-American males may dominate a number of collegiate and professional sports but they are still viewed in a negative light by the very fans who love them. As long as they are winning and bringing in millions of dollars in revenue, they are superficially accepted by white fans. For example, at a basketball game during half-time and at subsequent practices, the coach of the men's basketball team told the team he wanted the players to play like "niggers" on the court and wished he had more "niggers" on the basketball court. Similarly, Marge Schott, owner of the Cincinnati Reds, was accused of referring to African-American male members of the team as "million-dollar nigger, dumb, lazy nigger," and making the comment, "I'd rather have a trained monkey working for me than a nigger." Similarly, the basketball coach at Central Michigan University was terminated for allegedly calling players the "N"-word.[3] Years later, the N-word is used so frequently in professional sports that the NFL has proposed a 15-yard penalty for using the word on the field. Even in professional basketball, African-American male players cannot escape incidents of racism. In early 2014, Donald Sterling, owner of

DOI: 10.1057/9781137408433.0004

the Los Angeles Clippers, allegedly made taped racist comments about Magic Johnson and other African-Americans.[4] The NBA subsequently fined and banned him for life from the sport.

Various reports, studies, and surveys confirm that white Americans perceive basically every personality trait, physical characteristic, work ethic, and even the mere persona of African-American males as negative. The general sentiment is that African-American males have no desire to be productive citizens. They are less intelligent, are drug dealers and addicts, possess the propensity to be violent, are genetically flawed, engage in criminal activities, are members of gangs, and are rapists. This represents only a partial list of stereotypical biases directed at African-American males. A study by the U.S. Glass Ceiling Commission reports that:

> African-American men are stereotypically perceived as lazy/undisciplined/ always late/fail to pay their taxes/unqualified but protected by affirmative action/violent/confrontational/emotional/hostile/aggressive/unpredictable/ unable to handle stressful situations/threatening/demanding/militant/loud/ and less intelligent than other racial or ethnic groups.[5]

Stereotypical biases regarding African-American males' sexual prowess and their sexual desire for white women are also prevalent. General stereotypical biases and myths regarding the sexuality of African-American males were articulated by Justice Clarence Thomas during his confirmation hearing to be a Supreme Court Justice. Justice Thomas stated:

> [I]n this country when it comes to sexual conduct we still have underlying racial attitudes about black men... [L]anguage throughout my life, language about the sexual prowess of black men, language about the sexual organs of black men... these are charges that play into racist, bigoted, stereotypes and these are the kinds of charges that are impossible to wash off.[6]

Unfortunately, Justice Thomas' description of how the sexuality of African-American men is perceived by white America is true; the fall-out of these stereotypes has been used to exclude or limit employment opportunities for African-American males in the workplace, especially where white females are also employed.

Negative images of African-American men as being "bogeymen" and "predators" have become so prevalent that when African-American males are falsely accused of committing a vicious criminal act, law enforcement authorities and the public automatically assume they are guilty. For example, in 1989, Charles Stuart, a white male, alleged that

DOI: 10.1057/9781137408433.0004

an African-American male robber shot and killed his pregnant wife. The Boston police immediately rounded up African-American males in a predominantly African-American community who fit the general description. When Stuart became the prime suspect for killing his wife, he committed suicide.

One of the most notorious cases involved Susan Smith's false allegations in 1994 that a black man carjacked her and her two toddlers and drove around in a small southern town.[7] The stereotypical bias directed at black males, especially in the south, overshadowed any questions that the allegation could be false. Eight days later it was determined that she had intentionally killed her sons by allowing her car to drive into a lake. There are a number of other cases where African-American males have been falsely accused of a crime. Both incidents are reminiscent of the black male character in *To Kill a Mocking Bird* who was falsely accused of raping a white female.

African-American males have historically been victims of false allegations of rape, most recently on college campuses. White female students have made false allegations of rape against African-American males at a number of predominantly white universities. In these cases, the allegations of an African-American male raping a white female student proved to be a hoax; however, the racial stereotype of African-American males being rapists overshadowed any presumption of innocence until proven guilty.

America is primarily segregated by race; thus, many white Americans have no positive experiences with African-American males. White Americans typically draw their perceptions of African-American males from the media, the press, television,[8] and motion pictures which project African-American males as being violent and involved in some form of criminal activity.

A federal judge cited the following quote from a newspaper article which reflects the fear white Americans have of young African-American males:

> If you are white, what images comes to mind when you think about young black males? For many, it is that of a criminal. When some whites see a young black male on the street, they react by clutching their purses, increasing their walking speed, or telegraphing their discomfort in other ways. Each night in most major cities, local TV news flashes pictures of young black males who have committed criminal acts...handcuffed with head down, or shot dead in the gutter or in body bags, this negative image of young black America is tragically a part of the nation's consciousness.[9]

DOI: 10.1057/9781137408433.0004

The local news and even best-selling novels perpetuate negative stereotypes about African-American males. A passage from Terry McMillan's *Waiting to Exhale* captures the conversation between a group of African-American females discussing African-American males:

> They're not all with white girls, they're not all homosexuals, they're not all married, either. When you get right down to it, we're talking five, maybe ten percent. What about the rest? They're ugly, stupid, in prison, unemployed, crackheads, short, liars, unreliable, irresponsible, too possessive, dogs, shallow, boring, stuck in the sixties, arrogant, childish, wimps...too old and set in their ways.'"

It appears that when African-American males are projected on the screen as being violent, shiftless, or drug addicts,'' the results are higher ratings and bigger box office attendance and sales. As early as 1915, in D.W. Griffith's *Birth of a Nation*, negative images of African-American males were projected in motion pictures. Further, stereotypical images have been projected in other popular movies, such as *Boyz N the Hood, New Jack City, Juice, Training Day, Baby Boy, Hustle & Flow*, and *American Gangster*. If they are not portrayed as gangsters they are casted in comedy movies where they play brainless acting adults. On the other end of the spectrum are movies which although highly acclaimed, such as *Twelve Years a Slave, The Butler*, and *Driving Miss Daisy*, portray African-American males as servants, slaves, and generally powerless beings. These stereotypes fit perfectly in the paradigm in which African-American males are viewed and the limited type of roles in which African-American male actors are portrayed, and that Hollywood is willing to finance.

Hollywood appears to be more interested in making these types of movies, rather than portraying African-American males as hardworking, productive citizens. Of late, African-American filmmaker Tyler Perry has written and produced movies which portray African-Americans in a more realistic and balanced manner, but these movies are viewed primarily by African-Americans. The negative portrayals of African-American men in the media have left many white Americans, if not fearing all African-American males; they are highly uncomfortable around them.

The elicit verbiage in some rap and hip-hop music has also perpetuated negative stereotypical biases toward young African-American males who reside in urban areas. Unfortunately, young African-American rappers frequently use racially derogatory words which label and sanction the views of African-American males as predators.

DOI: 10.1057/9781137408433.0004

As a personal anecdote, while attending a national conference of law professors in Washington, D.C., I had an extensive conversation with one of the presenters, a white female law professor, regarding law school teaching. I was dressed in a conservative blue suit and tie. After that particular session, I changed into tennis shoes and jeans to look for souvenirs at a shop near the hotel. Approximately twenty minutes after my conversation with the professor, I passed her on the street as she walked away from the hotel. As she walked toward me, I noticed she moved to the opposite far edge of the sidewalk. As we came within talking distance, I stated, "Professor, your presentation was excellent." She never made eye contact with me and continued to cautiously pass, without any recognition of my existence. I turned and noticed her pace had picked up, almost to a slight run. I yelled, "Professor, it's me, Professor Weatherspoon." Hesitantly, she looked over her shoulder and gave a reluctant wave, and continued a brisk nervous walk. I recognized that the stereotypical biases of black men had overtaken her visions of me as a law-abiding citizen. Some would suggest that my race and sex were not a factor in this experience; others, as I do, would conclude that it had everything to do with my race and sex.

As an African-American male, I too have faced similar experiences in Manhattan when attempting to get a taxi in the evening hours. Not even my status as a law professor with an American Express card could separate me from stereotypical biases directed at black men by taxi drivers. Danny Glover, actor and civil rights activist, faced similar challenges in 1999 while hailing a taxi in Manhattan. His complaint of race discrimination led the City of New York's Taxi and Limo Commission to crack down on a set of regulatory reforms passed in 1996 known as Operation Refusal, which make it illegal for a taxi driver to discriminate against certain passengers for biased reasons.[12] Even in Atlanta, with a suit and tie on, taxi drivers have blatantly passed me by to pick up white male patrons. On one occasion as other African taxi drivers watched as I approached the taxi with a blue suit on and luggage, in the hot of July for a trip to the airport, I was suddenly passed by for a white male walking behind me. The taxi driver who witnessed the incident apologized and stated that he thought the driver who pulled off believed he will get a better tip from the white guy than me, "because Black guys don't give good tips." My corporate appearance could not shield me from discrimination, not even from other persons of color. Similarly, African-American men have been faced with the humiliation of being stopped and questioned by police

DOI: 10.1057/9781137408433.0004

while traveling through rural and suburban communities for no credible reason, other than that they are viewed as criminals.

Even the President of the United States, President Obama, faces similar stereotypical biases. He described them in this manner:

> There are very few African-American men in this country who haven't had the experience of being followed when they were shopping in a department store. That includes me. There are very few African-American men who haven't had the experience of walking across the street and hearing the locks click on the doors of cars. That happens to me, at least before I was a senator. There are very few African-Americans who haven't had the experience of getting on an elevator and a woman clutching her purse nervously and holding her breath until she had a chance to get off. That happens often.[13]

Stereotypical biases that negatively impact African-American males in employment include the criminal justice system, societal status, and acceptability by the majority of citizens. Even more compelling is the instinctive hatred of whites toward African-American males. Too often, this hatred has resulted in brutal beatings and the killing of African-American males, not only during slavery but also in the twenty-first century.

The brutal killing of an African-American male in Jasper, Texas, who was chained and dragged behind a pickup truck, as well as an African-American male in Newberry, South Carolina, who was dragged for more than 10 miles illustrate the violent acts of hatred that African-American males may face long after the end of slavery.

Notes

1 *Beauharnais v. Illinois*, 343 U.S. 250, 252 (1951).

2 Cindy Boren, *Richard Sherman Frustrated By Reaction, Equates "Thug" With Racial Slur, Wash. Post, the Early Lead* (January 23, 2014), www.washingtonpost.com.

3 *Dambrot v. Central Michigan University*, 55 F. 3d 12177 (1995).

4 Michael McCann, *What's Next For NBA in Donald Sterling Case From a Legal Standpoint?* (April 28, 2014, 4:59 PM), http://sportsillustrated.cnn.com/nba/news/20140426/donald-sterling-la-clippers-adam-silver-nba/. Clipper owner (last visited May 28, 2014).

5 *U.S. Glass Ceiling Commission, Good for Business: Making Full Use of the Nation's Human Capital* 71 (1995), *available at* http://www.dol.gov/dol/aboutdol/history/reich/reports/ceiling.htm.

DOI: 10.1057/9781137408433.0004

6   *Nominations of Judge Clarence Thomas to be Associate Justice of the Supreme Court of the United States*, 102d Cong. 201–202 (1991) (testimony of Judge Clarence Thomas).

7   *Racial Hoaxes: Black Men and Imaginary Crimes*, June 8, 2009, *available at* http://www.npr.org/templates/story/.php?storyId=105096024.

8   Darron T. Smith, *Images of Black Males in Popular Media*, Black Voices, March 14, 2013, *available at* http://www.huffingonpost.com/darron-t-smith-phd/black-men-media-b-2844990.html; Ronald E. Hall, *Clowns, Buffoons, and Gladiators: Media Portrayals of the African-American Man*, 1 J. MEN'S STUD. 239, 242–243 (1993) (describing how the media portrays African-American males); Charles M. Madigan, *Racial Stereotyping: An Old, Virulent Virus*, Chi. Trib., May 13, 1992, at 1C (finding that the media tends to focus on crime involving African-American males which perpetuates racial stereotyping).

9   *See United States v. Clary*, 846 F. Supp. 768, 771 (E.D. Mo. 1994); C. Thomas, *Media Overlooking Black-Success Stories*, St. Louis Post Dispatch, August 31, 1993, at 7B.

10   Terry Mcmillan, *Waiting to Exhale* 332 (Penguin Books 1992); Alice Walker, *Color Purple* (1982) (the lead African-American male character Mister was projected as being a child abuser and wife batterer).

11   *See generally Thelma Golden, Black Male: Representations of Masculinity in Contemporary American Art* (1994) (series of essays on how African-American males have been projected in art, films and by the media).

12   Taxicabs of New York City, *available at* http://en.wikipedia.org/wiki/Taxicabs_of_New_York_City#1990s_-_Changes_in_types_of_vehicles_and_Operation_Refusal.

13   *Floyd v. City of New York*, 959 F. Supp.2d 540, 587 (2013) (citing a speech by President Obama).

2

Racial Injustice in the Criminal Justice System

Abstract: *This chapter presents evidence that African-American males are disproportionately harmed by every aspect of the criminal justice system. From selective enforcement, incarceration, racial profiling, sentencing, prosecutorial abuse, police brutality, and to the death penalty, African-American males face racial injustices. The "war on drugs" has resulted in a disproportionate number of African-American males being arrested, sentenced, and incarcerated. The Federal Sentencing Guidelines have contributed to the mass number of African-American males in jail and prison. This chapter reveals that African-American males continue to face police brutality and disparity in the death penalty systems. This chapter offers compelling evidence that every African-American male in this country who drives a vehicle, or has traveled by bus or plane, either knowingly or unknowingly has been the victim of racial profiling by law enforcement officials. This chapter also discusses how African-American male youth are at risk of being arrested, detained, and prosecuted as adults.*

Weatherspoon, Floyd. *African-American Males and the U.S. Justice System of Marginalization: A National Tragedy*. New York: Palgrave Macmillan, 2014. DOI: 10.1057/9781137408433.0005.

African-American males are disproportionately harmed by every aspect of the criminal justice system. Specifically, African-American males are treated adversely from selective enforcement to incarceration to racial profiling, sentencing, prosecution, abuse, police brutality, and death penalty.[1] African-American males are targets of law enforcement. In theory, the American justice system is designed to ensure that each American's basic constitutional rights are preserved and protected. Most Americans, including African-Americans, believe that our justice system protects the constitutional rights of all Americans. The extent of protection, however, is viewed differently by whites. Indeed, African-Americans feel that their constitutional rights have been marginalized by the very system in place to protect their rights.

In particular, the criminal justice system has permitted and in some cases sanctioned the use of the immutable characteristic of race to be the motivating factor in the enforcement of public laws. Such actions or inactions on the part of individuals trusted with the enforcement of laws have served as a detriment to the dream that all Americans have inalienable rights. In other words, in their zealousness to enforce public laws, governmental officials have selected African-Americans, particularly males, on the basis of their race and gender to be stopped, arrested, charged, prosecuted, incarcerated, and put to death.

2.1 The mass incarceration of African-American males

Demographic Characteristics of Jail Inmates, 2009:

33.2% White Males, 39% Black Males, 3.5% White Females, 2.0% Black Females, 22.2% Other.

SOURCE: U.S. Department of Justice, Office of Justice Programs, Bureau of Justice Statistics, Prisoners in 2009, p. 27.

In a class discussion with law students in my African-American Males and the Law Seminar, I asked the students if they could think of an institutional system where mass numbers of individuals are involuntarily placed in servitude for extended periods of time or life. In addition, they lost the right to vote, to freely travel, to obtain an education, to gain meaningful employment, are more harshly punished than whites who committed the same crime, and are housed in deplorable conditions.

DOI: 10.1057/9781137408433.0005

Without hesitation, the law students responded that I was describing the institution of slavery in America or the period after Reconstruction. In reality, I was describing the present status of African-American males who are imprisoned in mass numbers. In fact, more African-American men are in jail now than those enslaved in 1850. The United States has one of the highest rates of prison populations in the world, with a rate of 762 per 100,000.[2] In addition, a 2010 study by the Pew Charitable Trust reported that 1 in 12 African-American males between the ages of 18 to 64 years were incarcerated, whereas 1 in 87 white males were incarcerated.[3] The U.S. Justice Department also reported that in 2012 African-American males who were sentenced under state and federal jurisdictions were 2,841 per 100,000, whereas white males were 463 per 100,000.[4] This illustrates how African-American males are disproportionately locked up in jails and prisons around the country.

Almost seven million U.S. adults are among the correction population. This number includes individuals who are on probation, on parole, in prisons, or in local jails.[5] African-American males are disproportionally represented at all stages of the correction system. Indeed, prisons in America have become a system of "warehousing" African-American males.[6]

The high rate of incarceration of African-American males is having a devastating impact on African-American communities and families.[7] The rate of incarceration of African-American males has both direct and indirect impacts on the African-American community, the society as a whole, and the overall status of African-American males, both socially and economically.[8]

The mass incarceration of African-American males has caused the absence of a father figure in the black family. Not only are fathers absent but so are uncles and male cousins who have traditionally taken on the role of mentor and role model when the father was absent. They too, however, are among the mass number of African-American males incarcerated, leaving African-American women as heads of households.

Moreover, the high incarceration rate of African-American males is a direct result of factors, that is, sentencing practices, selective enforcement, judicial biases, etc., discussed in other chapters of this book. Unfortunately, far too many lawyers who represent African-American males in criminal cases, and judges who hear these cases, perceive African-American males, particularly black youth, as dangerous and not worthy of rehabilitation. Thus, jail is where they should be forever

DOI: 10.1057/9781137408433.0005

stowed away from society. The Sentencing Commission has projected that if African-American males continue to be incarcerated at the present rate "one of every three black American male born today can expect to go to prison in his life, compared to one of every seventeen white males."[9]

Race plays a major role in how justice is administered in most state justice systems.[10] A number of states have finally taken initiatives to study where and how racism and ethnic bias impact the justice system. In Florida, for example, the Chief Justice of the Florida Supreme Court issued an order creating the Racial and Ethnic Bias Commission to determine whether race or ethnicity was a consideration in the administration of justice in Florida.

The Commission determined, in part, that minorities are underrepresented as judges and attorneys, minorities are subjected to police brutality, and minority juveniles are more harshly treated than nonminorities. The Commission also found that the typical criminal court session, where the defendant is an African-American male, involves predominantly white juries, judges, prosecutors, and defense counsel.

The State of Washington created a Task Force on Race and Criminal Justice System. The Task Force was organized after a member of the Supreme Court stated that "African-Americans are overrepresented in the prison population because they commit a disproportionate number of crimes."[11] The Task Force found "that much of disproportionality is explained by facially neutral policies that have racially disparate effects." Specifically, the Task Force found, in part, that:

▸ Youth of color in juvenile justice system face harsher sentencing outcomes than similarly situated white youth, as well as disparate treatment by probation officers.
▸ Defendants of color were significantly less likely than similarly situated white defendants to receive sentences that fell below the standard range.
▸ Among drug offenders, black defendants were 62% more likely to be sentenced to prison than similarly situated white defendants.[12]

A number of states have also established similar task forces to explore why African-American males are disproportionately incarcerated in state prisons. The State of Wisconsin, for example, completed a study on *Wisconsin's Mass Incarceration of African American Males: Workforce Challenges for 2013*, held in part that:

DOI: 10.1057/9781137408433.0005

In April of 2010 when the U.S. Census Bureau conducted its decennial count of Wisconsin residents, it found that 12.8% or (1 in 8) of African-American working age men behind bars in state prisons and local jails. This rate of mass incarceration is the highest for African American men in the country and nearly double the national average of 6.7 (or 1 in 15).[13]

The State of Maryland determined that African-American males only make up 28% of the state's population. However, they constitute 76% of the state prison population.[14] Even more disheartening is that in 2000 it was reported that half of all young African-American males in the Baltimore area were in some form of criminal justice system.[15]

Congress has also held hearings on why African-Americans, particularly black men, are disproportionately impacted by the criminal justice system. Members of Congress expressed concern that "approximately 2.3 million people are locked up in our nation's prison and jails, a 500 percent increase over the last 30 years."[16]

The number of African-Americans under the jurisdiction of the criminal justice system is almost too startling to state. In 2012, the U.S. Department of Justice reported the following imprisonment rate of African-American males:

▶ They are six times more likely to be incarcerated than white males.
▶ Their imprisonment rate is at least four times that of white males in all age groups.
▶ The Imprisonment rate of those aged 39 or younger is more than six times greater than that of white males.[17]

The high rate of incarceration of African-American males is having a devastating impact on the lives of African-American men at all ages. The actual numbers are even more telling of the enslavement of African-American males in prisons and jails. At the end of 2011, of the 1.5 million individuals sentenced under state and federal jurisdictions, 555,300 were African-American males.[18] In 2011, African-American males were disproportionately sentenced in all age groups, especially between the ages of 20 and 34 years.[19]

In addition, many states have invested billions of dollars in building new prisons, to house the flood of African-American males who are on track for incarceration. Indeed, some states have invested more in building prisons than in their educational system. There are no doubts that if the rate of incarceration continues, there will be a need for states to build additional prisons.

DOI: 10.1057/9781137408433.0005

The Sentencing Project has reported that approximately half a million black males are permanently disenfranchised to vote, as a result of state laws which limit the rights of felons to vote.[20] Further there is a decline in potential wages that black male youth earn after they have been incarcerated. It is interesting to note that in 2010, it cost Florida $31,307 to incarcerate each inmate for the year. Could the state use alternative means to punish, possibly to rehabilitate, thus saving tax payers billions of dollars?

The government's "war on drugs" has resulted in a disproportionate number of African-Americans sentenced to prison, especially when nearly half of the inmates in federal prisons are serving time for drug offenses.[21] It has been suggested that the "war on drugs" policy is a present-day Black Code which results in African-American males being targeted and sentenced to prison for an extended period of time.[22] If this trend continues, it is projected that there will be more African-American males in prison than were enslaved from 1820 to 1860. A report by the American Civil Liberties Union reported that:

> The number of black men in prison (792,000) has already equaled the number of men enslaved in 1820. With the current momentum of the drug war fueling an ever expanding prison – industrial complex, if current trends continue, only 15 years remain before the United States incarcerates as many African-American men as were faced into chattel bondage at slavery's peak, in 1860.[23]

Presently, there are more African-American males in prison than in college.[24] A study by the Justice Policy Institute reports that:

> In 2000, there were approximately 791,000 African American men under the jurisdiction of state and federal prison systems and in local jails. The same year, there were 603,000 African American men enrolled in higher education.

The recidivism rate for African-American males released from prison is also extremely high. Thus, the prison population continues to grow with new and returning African-American male inmates.[25] This revolving door of imprisonment of African-American males is comparable to slaves who escaped from slavery but were easily tracked down by slave owners and returned into slavery. Because other institutional policies prohibit the employment of individuals with criminal records and an education system which fails to train and educate African-American males, they often return to prison. This vicious cycle repeats itself over and over again.

2.1.1 Federal prison population of African-American males

The incarceration of inmates in federal prisons continues to rise at an alarming rate. As the numbers of inmates in some state prisons are decreasing, the opposite is true for federal prisons.[26] The U.S. Justice Department reported in 2012 that there were more than 200,000 inmates under the jurisdiction of the federal prison system, including inmates in privately managed federal facilities.[27] African-Americans represent approximately 40% of federal prisoners.[28]

African-American males face racial disparities in the federal system as it relates to sentencing, and time served. Similarly, there is evidence that African-American males received longer sentences than whites for violating the same federal laws. For example, African-Americans, particularly African-American males, are disproportionately impacted by federal sentencing policies.[29]

2.1.2 State imprisonment of African-American males

In 2012, the U.S. Department of Justice reported that 1,267,000 inmates were in the custody of state prisons.[30] It is also reported that states with the highest incarceration rate per 100,000 are Louisiana, Georgia, Texas, Mississippi, Oklahoma, Arkansas, Alabama, Florida, and South Carolina. Even more striking, the southern states have the highest incarceration rate of any other regions in the country. How ironic is it that the states with some of the highest rate of incarceration in the country are southern states where slavery was prevalent? The mass incarceration of African-American males in the South has the effect of creating state slave plantations.

The State of Louisiana has the highest rate of sentenced prisoners than any other state. It has a rate of 865 per 100,000 residents compared to Virginia with a rate of 464 and Mississippi with a rate of 685.[31] After Hurricane Katrina hit New Orleans in the summer of 2005, news reports vividly reported on the mass incarcerations of African-American males not only in local jails[32] throughout the state but also at the Angola Prison.[33] The Angola Prison houses 5,000 prisoners[34] of which 75% are African-Americans. The Angola Prison is one of the largest prisons in the country and has had a history of being one of the worst prisons in

DOI: 10.1057/9781137408433.0005

the country.[35] The prisoners at Angola were depicted in the Academy Award-nominated documentary, *Farm*.[36] Similar to blacks enslaved, it is reported that 85% of prisoners at Angola will never be released but will die while in prison.[37] What makes the Angola Prison so unique is that it was previously an 8,000 acre plantation where thousands of slaves provided free labor.[38] African-American males are disproportionately housed in other state prisons which have the reputation of abusing prisoners or maintaining a slavery environment.

The incarceration of African-Americans in state prisons starts even before they become adults. The Justice Department reports that between 1985 and 1997, African-American inmates under 18 years represented 58% of individuals under 18 years in state prisons.[39] From 1985 to 1997, the number of black and white males admitted under age 18 to state prisons more than doubled. In 1997, 4,300 black males under 18 entered State prison, as compared to 1,800 in 1985. Young African-American males who are placed in prison systems, probably for life, parallel young male slaves who faced a lifetime of slavery. They were born into a system of slavery and remained in slavery from their childhood to an adult life of enslavement.

The length of time African-American males serve in state prisons and jails has also grown. As a result of State truth-in-sentencing laws, inmates serve longer prison terms.[40] The laws require offenders to serve 85–88% of their sentence depending on the offense. The Violent Crime Control Act of 1994 provided for grants to states to build additional prisons and jails if they passed truth-in-sentencing laws.[41] A majority of states have passed truth-in-sentencing laws which have resulted in African-American males being incarcerated for longer periods of time, regardless of whether their behavior was good or not while in prison.

The enforcement of drug laws has had the greatest impact on the substantial increase in the incarceration of African-American males in state prisons.[42] During the past 15 years, states have promulgated three-strike laws that resulted in offenders being incarcerated for life after their third qualifying offense.[43] African-American male prisoners have been disproportionately impacted by these laws. The impact of the three-strike laws on decreasing crime has been negligible.[44]

The State of California used this law to incarcerate more than the other states. It has resulted in more than 80,000 individuals receiving mandatory sentences under the two/three-strike laws.[45] In 2009, the State of California prison population had grown to over 171,000.[46] The state

DOI: 10.1057/9781137408433.0005

acknowledged in 2005 "that prisons facilities can no longer adequately and safely accommodate the large number of inmates."[47] In 2011, the U.S. Supreme Court upheld the State of California plan to reduce its prison population to alleviate overcrowding.[48] As a result of the Supreme Court's decision and with state legislation, California now leads the way in reducing its prison population.

2.1.3 Local jails' population of African-American males

In 2012 more than 744,000 individuals were in local jails in the United States.[49]

African-Americans are disproportionately represented by 37% of those in local jails,[50] of which a majority were African-American males.[51] "More than fifty percent of all prisoners housed in local jails in 2011 were in serving time in Louisiana, Texas, or Tennessee."[52] Other states with high jail populations include Kentucky, Mississippi, and West Virginia.[53] As in previous surveys, African-American males, particularly those in their twenties and thirties, are disproportionately incarcerated in local jails.

2.1.4 Probation and parole: a revolving door

As the number of individuals incarcerated explodes so does the number of individuals on probation and parole. In 2012, approximately 4 million individuals in the United States were on probation.[54] A combination of individuals on probation or parole reached approximately 5 million.[55] As with other data on correctional populations, African-Americans disproportionately represented with 30% on probation[56] and 40% on parole.

2.1.5 Prison for profits: black male inmates industrial complex

The mass incarceration of African-American males is part of a 20 billion dollar prison industry.[57] The privately managed prison system is similar to slave owners who profited from slavery;[58] corporations have contracted with states and the federal governments to manage prisoners for profit. The numbers of private facilities continue to rise at an alarming rate. The present count of state and federal prisoners in private prisons at the end of 2000 was approximately 87,000.[59] In 2010, the number had grown to over 137,000 prisoners in private prisons.[60] The government use of private prisons, especially states, to house and supervise inmates has a long

DOI: 10.1057/9781137408433.0005

troubling history in America.[61] Often, that history reveals the abusive conduct in human treatment of inmates at the hands of private contractors.[62] The incarceration of African-American males supports an entire industry as they did during slavery when slaves were used to harvest cotton. The mass incarceration of African-American males provides for jobs,[63] building contracts, medical services, and purchases of products and services. Major corporations, in particular, benefit by the millions of individuals incarcerated by charging exorbitant fees for phone usage,[64] selling food products to feed prisoners, and the purchase of uniforms.[65] For example, in 2001, the U.S. Department of Justice reported that more than 200,000 individuals classified as staff were employed in jails and more than 150,000 were employed as correctional officers.[66] In addition, the Federal Bureau of Prisons employed approximately 15,000 correctional officers and 35,000 staff in 2003.[67] In May 2013, the Justice Department projected that approximately 500,000 correctional officers and jailers are employed at federal, state, and local facilities.[68] These numbers illustrate how the mass incarcerations of African-American males provide for large numbers of individuals to be employed in federal and state correctional systems. Even though this may not be illegal, it clearly raises ethical issues.

Unless the public demands a change in the mass criminalization of Americans, especially African-American males, their economic and social status will continue to be marginalized. Public policy makers, especially state legislatures, must revisit how drug policies have resulted in the mass number of their citizens to be incarcerated, costing taxpayers billions in prison expenses.

2.2   Racial profiling of African-American males

Every African-American male in this country who drives a vehicle, or has traveled by bus or plane, either knowingly or unknowingly has been the victim of racial profiling by law enforcement officials. Indeed, African-American males are disproportionately targeted, stopped, and searched by law enforcement officials based on race and gender. Those responsible for enforcement of public laws view African-American males as criminals. Unfortunately, the American justice system has condoned, supported, and in some instances encouraged such actions by law enforcement officials to stop, arrest, prosecute, and incarcerate

DOI: 10.1057/9781137408433.0005

African-American males. On the basis of race and gender, governmental officials have occasionally or inadvertently devised a profile of the typical criminal: black and male.

The term "driving while black" has been used to describe the practice of law enforcement officials to stop African-American drivers without probable cause.[69] The practice particularly targets African-American males. African-American males are singled out not only while driving, but also while schooling, eating, running for political office, walking, biking, banking, serving as a juror, getting a taxi, shopping, and just being black and a male. The mere fact of being black and male in America is sufficient cause for governmental and private law enforcement officials to abridge the rights of African-American males.

The Court in *Washington v. Lambert*[70] expressed concerns of how general descriptions of an African-American male suspect can lead to a significant number of African-Americans being stopped and detained. The court stated that "a significant percentage of African-American males walking, eating, going to work or to a movie, ball game or concert, with a friend or relative, might well find themselves subjected to similar treatment, at least if they are in a predominately white neighborhood."[71] This is not to suggest that law enforcement officers can never consider race when performing their job; in fact, it is just the opposite. For example, where a witness identifies the race and gender of a suspect, it is relevant evidence to consider in an effort to apprehend a criminal. Racial profiling, however, involves a predisposition held by law enforcement officers who are members of the majority, to believe that minorities, particularly African-American males, are engaged in criminal activities; therefore, they are stopped and searched without probable cause or reasonable suspicion. The U.S. Department of Justice defines racial profiling as a practice which at its core concerns the invidious use of race or ethnicity as a criterion in conducting stops, searches, and other law enforcement investigative procedures. It is premised on the erroneous assumption that any particular individual of one race or ethnicity is more likely to engage in misconduct than any particular individual of another race or ethnicity.

Racial profiling has been institutionalized into our American justice system, as well as other systems that disproportionately exclude, punish, and ostracize African-American males. For example, racial profiling on the part of governmental officials has encouraged and, to a certain extent, licensed individuals in the private sector to devise similar racial

DOI: 10.1057/9781137408433.0005

profiles based on stereotypical biases to selectively punish and exclude African-American males from employment opportunities.

2.2.1   Targeting African-American males

African-American males are the primary victims of racial profiling in this country. Moreover, African-American males believe they are the primary victims of racial profiling in this country. Surveys conducted by the Washington Post and the Black America's Political Action Committee ("BAMPAC") determined that almost 50% of African-American males surveyed believed they had been victims of racial profiling. The practice of racial profiling is not limited to just urban areas. Indeed, it happens wherever African-American males live, work, or traverse; whether in cities, rural communities, East or West, North or South, they face closer scrutiny by law enforcement officials than white males. Racial profiling of African-American males is not a new phenomenon but a repackaging of a twentieth-century form of racial discrimination toward black males. Justice Marshall said it best when he faced racial profiling in the 1960s:

> white man came up beside me in plain clothes with a great big pistol on his hip. And he said, "Nigger boy, what are you doing here?" And I said, "Well I'm waiting for the train to Shreveport." And he said, "There's only one more train comes through here, and that's the 4 o'clock, and you'd better be on it because the sun is never going down on a live nigger in this town."[72]

At a different time and in a different place, African-American males were, and remain, singled out for harassment. Interestingly, racial profiling is not isolated to just black male youths in urban areas with a "gangster" or "rapper" appearance or demeanor. Racial profiling is applied in a nondiscriminatory manner among African-American males, regardless of their economic status. African-American males who are lawyers, educators, sport figures, legislators, actors, news reporters, and business executives are stopped, questioned, and humiliated by law enforcement officers simply because they are black and male. One-thousand dollar Armani suits do not shield them from being perceived as drug-dealing thugs.

Negative stereotypical biases of African-American males overshadow any appearances that they are law-abiding citizens. Indeed, in the eyes of many law enforcement officers, an African-American male driving a Mercedes Benz projects the presumption of illegal activity, not the presumption of a hard-working citizen.

DOI: 10.1057/9781137408433.0005

2.2.2   The impact of stereotypical biases on racial profiling

Stereotypical biases directed at African-American males by law enforcement officials have resulted in a disproportionate number of African-American males being stopped and searched. Racial profiling due to stereotypical biases also has a direct correlation to the high incarceration rate of African-American males, especially those between the ages of 20 and 39 years. It is presupposed by many law enforcement officials that young African-American males are engaged in criminal activities, especially drug-dealing. This sentiment by many law enforcement officers became evident when the Chief of New Jersey Troopers defended racial profiling by stating that "mostly minorities" were engaged in the trafficking of marijuana and cocaine. It should be obvious that if law enforcement agencies focus the enforcement of drug laws toward African-American males, and ignore whites based on stereotypical biases, African-American males will be disproportionately stopped and searched. Thus, it will appear they are the only segment of the country's population engaged in criminal drug activities. In turn, the data from one jurisdiction will be relied on by another jurisdiction to justify the racial profiling of African-American males; thus, the discriminatory conduct is perpetuated.

The mere appearance, talk, walk, and dress of African-American males are viewed in a negative light by many white Americans. Moreover, African-American males who travel through white neighborhoods may find themselves stopped and pulled over by law enforcement officials and investigated. For example, two African-American males and a white male were stopped as they passed through the City of Torrance, a predominately white suburb of Los Angeles. The court, in upholding the jury award of $245,000 in compensatory and punitive damages, stated:

> The police officers in this case appear to have chosen the wrong young people. Two African American teens and a white teen were innocently driving through the City of Torrance, happily and quietly celebrating their graduation from prep school. For no good reason, two police officers stopped their car without probable cause or reasonable suspicion, conducted an illegal search of the vehicle, and used degrading and excessive force on the young boys. Such is not an isolated incident in the Greater Los Angeles area, or across the country. This time, however, the youngsters had the wherewithal and families with the legal knowledge and economic resources to seek justice for the wrongs committed. The defendants received a fair and impartial trial.[73]

DOI: 10.1057/9781137408433.0005

African-American males who drive foreign sports or luxury cars are almost certain to be stopped by law enforcement for suspicion of drug trafficking or car theft. As a result of discriminatory stops, African-American males are disproportionately arrested by law enforcement officers. Negative images of this group and stereotypical biases directed at its members may automatically lead to them being stopped and arrested. Due to such biases, law enforcement officials assume that every African-American male is a threat to them, and to society.

The targeting of minorities for traffic stops, especially young African-American and Hispanic males, may enhance their sentence for other crimes, if the traffic violation is considered in determining their penalty. Unfortunately, the killing of African-American males by law enforcement officials may also have a direct correlation to the percentage of African-Americans being stopped.

2.2.3   Traffic stops: driving while black and male

More than thirty years ago, the U.S. Supreme Court in *Terry v. Ohio*[74] placed limitations on the ability of enforcement officers to stop and search individuals without reasonable suspicion that they were engaged in criminal activity. Reasonable suspicion must be based on something more than an "inchoate and particularized suspicion or hunch."[75] In addition, the Supreme Court held in the *United States v. Sokolow*[76] that "police conduct carried out solely on the basis of imprecise stereotypes of what criminals look like, or on the basis of irreverent personal characteristics such as race" violates the Fourth Amendment. Law enforcement officers are required to have "specific and articulable facts."

Even though these limitations are part of the criminal justice jurisprudence and have been tested repeatedly in court, law enforcement officers have use racial profiling as a means to routinely stop and search African-American males. African-American males who are stopped and searched will often allege that the search and seizure violated their Fourth Amendment rights; thus, the evidence seized must be suppressed at trial. Because the standard for an investigatory stop does not require probable cause, but only reasonable suspicion, courts have consistently denied the suppression of such evidence.

The use of racial profiling in the selective enforcement of public laws is most evident in traffic stops by law enforcement officers. It can also be a most humiliating and frightening experience for anyone, especially

African-American males, who may fear imminent harm from police officers. For example, in *Flowers v. Fiore*,[77] an African-American male motorist alleged that law enforcement officers engaged in racial profiling when he was stopped, handcuffed, forced to his knees, and had his car searched. According to the police officers, they stopped Flowers because a resident called the police and stated that he received a call from someone who purported to be sending over "two black guys with a gun." Shortly thereafter, the police observed Flowers driving past the caller's house. The police stopped him, searched his car, and then released him because there was no evidence that he was sent to harm the resident.

Flowers sued under various federal and state laws, alleging in part that the police engaged in racial profiling, stopping him in violation of his rights under the Equal Protection Clause of the Fourteenth Amendment. The Court granted the defendants' motion for summary judgment because in the eyes of the court the search was reasonable. The court stated that innocent victims will be at times subjected to such stops by police officers and suggested that Flowers was entitled to a "good explanation and an apology." The court failed to recognize that too often the "innocent victims," who were being stopped and humiliated by law enforcement officers, were African-American males.

The court in *Washington v. Lambert* acknowledged the following:

> In this nation, all people have a right to be free from the terrifying and humiliating experience of being pulled from their cars at gunpoint, handcuffed, or made to lie face down on the pavement when insufficient reason for such intrusive police conduct exists.[78]

Unfortunately, African-American males are treated in this manner by law enforcement officials, without consciousness of, or concerns about their constitutional rights.

One of the most egregious examples of racial profiling of African-American males occurred in 1998 when two New Jersey Troopers stopped and fired eleven times at a van traveling on the New Jersey Turnpike, wounding three of the passengers. The van was occupied by three African-American males and a Hispanic male, all from New York, who were en route to North Carolina to try out for a baseball team. The shooting brought national attention to the practice of stopping African-Americans, particularly African-American males, without probable cause or reasonable suspicion that they were engaged in a criminal activity.

DOI: 10.1057/9781137408433.0005

Similarly, in *State v. Soto*,[79] a superior court judge in Gloucester County, New Jersey, granted the defendant's motion to suppress evidence seized after being stopped on the New Jersey Turnpike. The court held that the 17 minority defendants who were African-Americans, the majority of whom were males, established a case of selective enforcement based on race. In *Soto*, the defense conducted a study to determine if law enforcement officers were engaged in racial profiling. The study revealed that "an adult black male was present in 88% of the cases where the gender of all occupants could be determined and that where gender and age could be determined, a black male 30 or younger was present in 63 of the cases."[80]

Other examples of racial profiling include an incident involving the Maryland State Police, which settled a lawsuit following the discovery of an internal memo that encouraged state troopers to target African-American males driving east on I-68. The profile of the Maryland State Police suggested that being black plus male and driving on I-68 equaled criminal activity.

During the past ten years, a number of studies support the conclusion that the race and color of drivers has been the basis for state law enforcement officers to stop and search cars driven by African-Americans, particularly African-American males. One of the most comprehensive and widely circulated studies on racial profiling was conducted in 1999 to determine whether the state police in New Jersey engaged in racial profiling on the New Jersey Turnpike. The study concluded that minorities were disproportionately stopped and treated differently than white motorists. Officials of the U.S. Department of Justice and the State of New Jersey ultimately signed a consent decree to prohibit and prevent racial profiling by the New Jersey State Police.

Further, a study in Maryland revealed that during a three-year review of motorists stopped on I-95, African-Americans represented 70% of individuals stopped by the police, even though African-Americans made up only about 17% of motorists. A similar study of traffic stops in Missouri also revealed that African-Americans were disproportionately stopped and searched. Additionally, a study by the Orlando Sentinel concluded that African-Americans and Hispanics represented a small percentage of motorists on a particular Florida highway; however, they represented almost 70% of individuals stopped and 80% of those whose cars were actually searched. In parts of Oklahoma, African-Americans are disproportionately stopped and convicted of traffic violations.

DOI: 10.1057/9781137408433.0005

A 2008 study of traffic stop data in Arizona found that "Hispanics and Blacks received the highest percentage of citations and Hispanic, Native Americans and Black drivers were all significantly more likely than white drivers to be arrested and searched."[81] A 2012 study of traffic stops in North Carolina determined that:

> While Blacks make up 22% of the overall population, they constitute 30% of those pulled over, 33% of people pulled over for "other vehicle" issues, 37% of those pulled over for "vehicle equipment "issues and 38% of those stopped for "vehicle regulatory" issues.
>
> Blacks are 77 percent more likely to be searched, given a traffic stop, than Whites.[82]

In January of 2014, Northeastern University reported the outcome of a study on traffic stops in Rhode Island. The study revealed in part, that:

> When looking at stops of residents compared to the residential population, the analysis found that 23 communities stopped more non-white residents than would have been expected given the census population. In four communities the disparity is greater than 10% and merit further consideration.[83]

Similar studies of city law enforcement officials find that minorities are also disproportionately stopped. For example, the Salt Lake Tribune conducted a study of traffic tickets issued by the Salt Lake City Police Department. The survey revealed that African-Americans were twice as likely as white drivers to receive a traffic ticket. In Milwaukee, a study of 46,000 traffic stops determined that African-American drivers were seven times more likely to be stopped by the city police than white drivers.[84] In San Diego, a study of the Police Department revealed that African-Americans and Hispanics were more likely than whites, and Asian-Americans to be stopped. In Suffolk County, New York, as part of an investigative report, a white motorist and a black motorist were sent to travel throughout the county. The results were not a surprise that African-American male motorists were "consistently pulled over, while Caucasians were not."[85]

There is also some evidence that the controversial "stop and frisk" law of New York primarily targets young African-American males. Specifically, the New York Civil Liberties Union reported that in 2010, the enforcement of the City's stop-and-frisk program resulted in more than 700,000 individuals being stopped and frisked by the New York Police Department. The report revealed that young African-American

DOI: 10.1057/9781137408433.0005

and Latino males were disproportionately stopped in 2011. Specifically the report found that:

> Young black and Latino males were the targets of a hugely disproportionate number of stops in 2011. While black and Latino males between the ages of 14 and 24 account for only 4.7 percent of the city's population, they accounted for 41.6 percent of those stopped. By contrast, white males between the ages of 14 and 24 make up 2 percent of the city's population but account for 3.8 percent of stops. Remarkably, the number of stops of young black men last year actually exceeded the total number of young black men in the city (168,126 as compared to 158,406).[86]

In response to New York City's stop-and-frisk policy, the City was sued in *Floyd v. New York City*.[87] In 2013, Judge Shira A. Scheindlin held that:

> [t]he City is liable for violating plaintiffs' Fourth and Fourteenth Amendment rights. The City acted with deliberate indifference toward the NYPD's practice of making unconstitutional stops and conducting unconstitutional frisks. Even if the City had not been deliberately indifferent, the NYPD's unconstitutional practices were sufficiently widespread as to have the force of law. In addition, the City adopted a policy of indirect racial profiling by targeting racially defined groups for stops based on local crime suspect data. This has resulted in the disproportionate and discriminatory stopping of blacks and Hispanics in violation of the Equal Protection Clause. Both statistical and anecdotal evidence showed that minorities are indeed treated differently than whites.[88]

Before the decision could be implemented a three-judge panel on the Second Circuit removed Judge Scheindlin from the case and issued a stay of the remedies she had ordered. The Court of Appeals for the Second Circuit held that "these cases shall be assigned to a different District Judge, chosen randomly under the established practices of the District Court for the Southern District of New York." The Court determined that the District Judge ran afoul of the Code of Conduct for U.S. Judges, Canon 2. The Court further determined that "the appearance of impartiality surrounding this litigation was compromised by the District Judge's improper application of the Court's related case rule."[89]

These incidents support the suspicions held by African-American males that their rendezvous with the police have not occurred by chance, but instead because of the darkness of their skin and their gender. African-American males are targets of invidious and systematic discrimination from local law enforcement authorities when they travel in predominately

DOI: 10.1057/9781137408433.0005

white communities. Cities have engaged in a practice of stopping and ticketing blacks who enter the city, particularly black males.

One of the most egregious selective enforcement cases involved George Murphy, an African-American male, who made the mistake of traveling to Reynoldsburg, Ohio, to meet a friend. He was followed by a Reynoldsburg police officer who pulled him over a short distance from his hotel. After Murphy was arrested and charged with driving under a suspended license, cocaine was found in the car. Felony charges were brought against him, but a jury failed to convict him. Murphy subsequently brought suit against the city after learning of an internal investigation of some officers for racial prejudice. The internal investigation discovered that within the police department, there was a group of white police officers that called themselves members of SNAT ("Special Nigger Arrest Team"). Murphy alleged that the team engaged in selective enforcement against blacks. After the case was dismissed by a lower court, the Ohio Supreme Court ordered the lower court to rehear Murphy's case.[90] The case was subsequently settled. This case illustrates how racial profiling by law enforcement officers can be intentional and by design.

Often, police officers may allege there is a legitimate reason for stopping African-American males, which in reality is a pretext to discrimination. An officer, for example, may use a state car seat belt law as a pretext to stop African-American males who may not use seat belts to the extent of white motorists. Officers also cite the failure to signal when changing lanes, or following too closely, or no reflector on a bike as a basis for a stop, and ultimately a search.

Incidents of racial profiling of African-American men continue to be reported, as law enforcement officials exercise their authority to stop and search law-abiding African-American male motorists in a discriminatory manner. This was illustrated in testimony given by Rossano Gerald, a decorated sergeant of the Gulf War. Sergeant Gerald testified before a subcommittee of Congress on the End of Racial Profiling Act of 2001. Sergeant Gerald testified how he was handcuffed and humiliated by a State Trooper while driving with his son in Oklahoma. Sergeant Gerald filed suit against the Oklahoma Highway Patrol after he was stopped twice in the same day. During the second stop he was detained for almost two hours while officers searched his car for drugs. Finding no drugs, he was given a warning ticket for failure to signal when changing a lane. The case subsequently settled for $75,000.[91]

DOI: 10.1057/9781137408433.0005

Ironically, there is evidence that the use of racial profiling is also used by white police officers to stop African-American male police officers who are off-duty. In a survey of 400 African-American police officers of the Milwaukee Police Department conducted by the University of Wisconsin-Milwaukee, in which 158 of those officers responded, the officers indicated that approximately one in three African-American male officers stated that they had been victims of racial profiling during the past year.

There is also evidence that African-American male officers who refuse to engage in racial profiling may also face reprisal, including termination. An incident in Providence, Rhode Island, exemplifies the ultimate negative result of a law enforcement officer engaging in racial profiling. An off-duty African-American male police officer witnessed a confrontation with an armed man, and went to assist two white police officers. The off-duty African-American male officer was shot and killed by the two white officers. The two officers stated that they did not recognize the officer who approached them with his gun drawn.

The U.S. Supreme Court decision in *Whren v. United States*[92] practically legitimizes the use of racial profiling by police officers. In *Whren*, two African-American males, driving a dark Pathfinder truck with temporary license plates, were pursued by plainclothes vice-squad officers after the driver failed to give a turning signal and sped off at an "unreasonable" speed. When the driver stopped at a red light, the officer approached the driver's door, and observed two large plastic bags of what appeared to be crack cocaine in the driver's hand. Both individuals were arrested and subsequently charged with violating various federal drug laws.

The petitioners challenged the legality of the stop and the seizure of the drugs. The district court denied the suppression motion and they were convicted. The Court of Appeals affirmed the convictions.

After reviewing a series of Fourth Amendment cases, the Supreme Court stated:

> [W]e think these cases foreclose any argument that the constitutional reasonableness of traffic stops depends on the actual motivations of the individual officers involved. We of course agree with petitioners that the Constitution prohibits selective enforcement of the law based on considerations such as race. But the constitutional basis for objecting to intentionally discriminatory application of laws is the Equal Protection Clause, not the Fourth Amendment. Subjective intentions play no role in ordinary, probable-cause Fourth Amendment analysis.[93]

DOI: 10.1057/9781137408433.0005

The *Whren* decision sanctions law enforcement officers to stop and question any motorist, ostensibly for an insignificant traffic violation, and subsequently charge them with other serious crimes, even though they have no reasonable cause to suspect the individual was engaged in a felony. It is irrelevant that the officer may have an "ulterior motive" or had "subjective intention" when making the stop. Even though it is difficult to prove, often the real reason for the stop is based on stereotypical biases that an African-American male is engaged in illegal drug activities. In *Kearse v. State*,[94] Judge Griffen, in a concurring opinion denying the motions to suppress evidence seized at the stop, stated in part:

> For countless African-American and Hispanic drivers, the prospect of being stopped for a traffic offense and asked to consent to a search of their vehicles has become part of the preparation for driving…I hope that police agencies will voluntarily discontinue the "highly disturbing" practice of suspecting that African-American and Hispanic motorists are more likely to be drug dealers and couriers so as to warrant being stopped for traffic offenses[,] so that their vehicles can be searched and their cash seized.[95]

Often, African-American males who are stopped based on a "reasonable suspicion" of a traffic violation are lined up along the highway, humiliated, and searched without probable cause. In proposing the End Racial Profiling Act of 2001, Congress made the following finding regarding racial profiling: "Racial profiling harms individuals subjected to it because they experience fear, anxiety, humiliation, anger, resentment, and cynicism when they are unjustifiably treated as criminal suspects." The Act has not passed Congress, after a number of attempts. More than a decade later, in 2013, with little hope of passage, the Act was again proposed to address the issue of racial profiling.[96]

Years later, the *Whren* decision continues to abridge the rights of African-American males. For example, in *Leftridge v. Matthews*,[97] two African-American males were stopped and frisked and alleged their race was the factor why the white police officers stopped them on the highway. Again, based on *Whren*, the court dismissed the claim but acknowledged the following type of humiliation that African-American drivers may face:

> Many law abiding people would feel violated at having to endure a frisk a drug dog scan, and a search of ones' vehicle in the middle of the night on the side of a highway. And, I recognize that Mr. Leftridge suspected a racial motive for the traffic stop. But, a lawsuit must be built on fact and not suspicion.[98]

DOI: 10.1057/9781137408433.0005

Such actions should undoubtedly be considered a violation of their Fourth Amendment rights. Furthermore, if the law enforcement officer detains the motorist longer than necessary to determine whether a traffic violation has occurred, or searches the car without consent or probable cause, the Fourth Amendment may be violated. Unfortunately, the *Whren* decision can be compared with the Supreme Court's decision in *Dred Scott v. Sanford*.⁹⁹ The *Dred Scott* decision resulted in African-Americans being denied their constitutional rights as citizens. Even though the cases are more than a hundred years apart, the impact of *Whren* on African-American males may be the same as *Dred Scott*. In *Dred Scott*, Judge Taney stated that a "[black man] had no rights which the white man was bound to respect." The U.S. Supreme Court decision in *Whren* raises questions of whether African-American men have certain constitutional rights.

2.2.4   Airport stops: drug courier profile

Most Americans, black and white, would agree there is an urgent need to "get tough on crime" in our country, particularly the elimination of the sale, use, and distribution of illegal drugs. In the late 1980s, the federal government declared "war on drugs" and appointed a drug czar to implement such policies. The "war on drugs," however, has resulted in a disproportionate number of African-American males being arrested, sentenced, and incarcerated. The mere fact that African-American males are being incarcerated for violating drug laws is not the issue. The concern is that African-American communities are the primary targets of drug enforcement sweeps, and that African-American males are the primary individuals targeted for arrest—normally receiving harsher sentencing for the same or similar offenses committed by whites. In fact, the "war on drugs" has almost become synonymous with policing the African-American community and black males.¹⁰⁰ White suburbs are less likely to be targeted even though the National Institute for Drug Abuse and other studies report that, although minorities represent a larger number of all individuals arrested for a drug violation, they represented a smaller number of individuals using illicit drugs.¹⁰¹

In many cases, the immutable characteristic of being a black male is considered a sufficient basis for law enforcement officers to have probable cause to stop African-American male motorists for interrogation. This is not to imply that drug laws should not be enforced in the African-American communities; however, African-American communities

DOI: 10.1057/9781137408433.0005

should not be disproportionately targeted for enforcement. African-American males should not be more severely punished for violating drug laws than whites.

The use of drug courier profiling is also used at airports, at bus stations, and with other modes of transportation to stop and search African-American males. African-American males have alleged racial profiling not only when driving a car, but when traveling by Amtrak and even when riding a bicycle. As an African-American male who travels by plane on a frequent basis, I am normally one of three or four African-Americans on the plane. My personal observation is that the percentage of airplane travelers that are African-American is extremely small. For example, a federal district court in Kentucky determined that "airplane passengers nationwide are estimated at 88% white, 5% African-American, and 1% Hispanic."[102] However, a review of statistics on African-Americans who are stopped, searched, and arrested by the U.S. Drug Enforcement Administration ("DEA") reveals that African-Americans are disproportionately stopped.[103]

In *United States v. Jennings*,[104] the officer acknowledged that half of his airport stops involved African-American or Hispanic passengers. However, the defendant points out that African-Americans and Hispanics "comprise far less than fifty percent of the airline passengers." The Constitution guarantees the right to travel without governmental interference. Although this right is enjoyed without thought by most Americans, African-American males are routinely stopped and singled out for interrogation, detainment, arrest, searches, and prosecution by the Drug Enforcement Administration's ("DEA") practice of stopping African-American male passengers at airports and bus stations to determine whether they are transporting drugs.

The DEA has developed what is known as "drug courier profiles." In *United States v. Elmore*,[105] a DEA agent provided the following characteristics of a drug courier profile:

> The seven primary characteristics are: (1) arrival from or departure to an identified source city; (2) carrying little or no luggage, or large quantities of empty suitcases; (3) unusual itinerary, such as rapid turnaround time for a very lengthy airplane trip; (4) use of an alias; (5) carrying unusually large amounts of currency in the many thousands of dollars, usually on their person, in briefcases or bags; (6) purchasing airline tickets with a large amount of small denomination currency; and (7) unusual nervousness beyond that ordinarily exhibited by passengers. The secondary characteristics are (1) the almost

DOI: 10.1057/9781137408433.0005

exclusive use of public transportation, particularly taxicabs, in departing from the airport; (2) immediately making a telephone call after deplaning; (3) leaving a false or fictitious call-back telephone number with the airline being utilized; and (4) excessively frequent travel to source or distribution cities.[106]

Even though the profile appears to be neutral on its face, the question still remains whether there are code words within these "neutral" terms that law enforcement officers interpret and manipulate to reach African-American travelers, particularly African-American males. It appears from previous federal cases that this list is ever-expanding. Justice Marshall expressed concern in *United States v. Sokolow*[107] that reliance on a profile of drug courier characteristics may subject innocent individuals to unwarranted police harassment and detention, especially since the profile has a "chameleon-like way of adapting to any particular set of observations."[108] These characteristics appear to be race-neutral and had race been listed, it would have raised constitutional concerns (e.g., a violation of the Equal Protection Clause of the Constitution). African-American males, in particular, view law enforcement officials with suspicion and distrust. The practice of drug courier profiling of African-American men further perpetuates the conflict between African-American males and law enforcement officials.

The enforcement of the "drug courier profile" by law enforcement officers has resulted in African-American males being detained, searched, humiliated, and embarrassed while exercising their constitutional right to travel. Based on the disproportionate number of African-American males stopped, it appears that the government's profile of a drug courier has become in practice the black male drug courier profile.

Courts have become suspicious of the use of the drug courier profile; however, the Court has failed to address the disparity in a manner to ensure equity in the enforcement of drug laws. For example, in *Jones v. United States Drug Enforcement Administration*,[109] minority passengers arriving at the Nashville Airport alleged racial profiling. The court stated "[i]t is clear from the testimony that [the] officers approached the travelers because of their race."[110] Moreover, Jones presented evidence of other incidents where African-Americans were stopped and interrogated, including a producer with the CBS news show "60 Minutes," without probable cause. Nevertheless, the court refused to grant Jones's request for injunctive relief against the DEA.

DOI: 10.1057/9781137408433.0005

This practice of stopping and searching African-American males is also enforced at bus terminals. A review of these practices by Congress is warranted to ensure that the constitutional rights of African-American males are protected. They should not be singled out for a stop and search because they are black and male.

In *United States v. Travis*,[111] the evidence clearly supported the conclusion that airport detectives targeted African-American travelers by using a race-based profile. The evidence presented by the defendants indicated that in 1992, 20 of the 21 individuals arrested at the Kentucky airport were of African-American or Hispanic descent. Even though the court expressed concerns that African-Americans may be targeted for searches at the airport, it nevertheless upheld the search as being lawful.

Further, in *United States v. Weaver*,[112] a DEA agent stopped an African-American male at the Kansas City International Airport, because "he was a roughly dressed young black male who might be a member of a Los Angeles street gang that had been bringing narcotics into the Kansas City area." Even with this evidence, the Eighth Circuit Court of Appeals, nevertheless, affirmed the district court's decision denying Weaver's motion to suppress evidence obtained by the government when he was stopped. In affirming the lower court's decision, the court of appeals acknowledged that had the decision to stop the African-American male been based solely on his race, the Constitution would have been violated.

The court, however, focused on the fact that the DEA agent also relied on race-neutral evidence to stop and question Weaver. Based on this analysis, law enforcement officers can easily circumvent the constitutional rights of African-American males by connecting racial factors with race-neutral factors in their decision to stop any individual. At the same time the Eighth Circuit stated that it agreed with the dissent, "that large groups of our citizens should not be regarded by law enforcement officers as presumptively criminal based on race." The dissenting judge stated, in part that "[o]ne of the most disturbing aspects of this case is the agents' reference to Weaver as a roughly dressed young black male." The dissent also expressed concern that the "[u]se of race as a factor simply reinforces the kind of stereotyping that lies behind drug courier profiles. When public officials begin to regard large groups of citizens as presumptively criminal, this country is in a perilous situation indeed." Nevertheless, African-American males who travel by plane or other modes of transportation may automatically be suspected of engaging in

DOI: 10.1057/9781137408433.0005

illegal activities solely based on the color of their skin. Proving that the DEA or other law enforcement officials are engaged in racial profiling in the enforcement of drug laws is almost impossible.

The Supreme Court decision in *Whren* gave law enforcement officers the authority to stop African-American males, and other minorities, on the basis of their race, and the Supreme Court decision in *United States v. Armstrong*[113] made it virtually impossible to prove that law enforcement officers were intentionally engaged in stopping African-American males. For all practical purposes, Armstrong gave law enforcement officials unfettered authority to profile, stop, chase, and prosecute African-Americans, particularly black males during the "war on drugs." If there was a case where the statistical data clearly supported a pattern and practice of selective enforcement on the basis of race, it would have been *Armstrong*.

In *Armstrong*, "the Federal Bureau of Alcohol, Tobacco, and Firearms and the Narcotics Division of Inglewood, California, Police Department had infiltrated a suspected crack distribution ring by using three confidential informants." As a result of the drug sting, Armstrong and other African-American males were indicted. Defendants filed a motion for discovery or for dismissal of the indictment alleging that the government had engaged in selective prosecution on the basis of race. To support their claim, they submitted an affidavit of an employee of the office of the Federal Public Defender described as stating:

> in every one of the 24 § 841 or § 846 [drug] cases closed by the office during 1991, the defendant was black. Accompanying the affidavit was a "study" listing the 24 defendants, their race, whether they were prosecuted for dealing cocaine as well as crack, and the status of each case.[114]

Over objections by the Government, the District Court granted the motion for discovery. After appeals to the Ninth Circuit, the Supreme Court granted certiorari to establish the standard for discovery for a selective prosecution claim. The Supreme Court acknowledged that the government is prohibited from using race as a basis to prosecute. From there, the Court established a heightened standard which ties the hands of defendants from discovering evidence to support their claim of selective enforcement. The Supreme Court held that to establish a selective prosecution claim, the claimant:

> Must demonstrate that the federal prosecutorial policy "had a discriminatory effect and that it was motivated by a discriminatory purpose." To establish

DOI: 10.1057/9781137408433.0005

a discriminatory effect in a race case, the claimant must show that similarly situated individuals of a different race were not prosecuted.[115]

The Supreme Court also held that this standard even applies when defendants are seeking discovery to prove their claim. The difficulty in selective enforcement cases is identifying whites who are treated more favorably by the prosecutor in the enforcement of drug laws.[116] The Court incorrectly hypothesized that the "similarly situated" standard will not make selective prosecution claims impossible to prove.[117] Subsequent selective enforcement cases, where a discovery motion to discover evidence to support "similarly situated" whites were treated more favorably, have been denied based on the Court's decision in Armstrong, thus leaving defendants, especially African-American male defendants, without sufficient evidence to support their claim.

The difficulty in meeting the *Armstrong* standard is illustrated in *United States v. Barlow*.[118] Barlow, an African-American male, was stopped by DEA agents at Chicago's Union Station after he purchased two one-way tickets to Topeka, Kansas. The DEA agents indicated that Barlow and his companion were stopped because they "kept glancing over their shoulders at the agents and whispering to one another." After receiving consent to search their bags, the DEA agents found drugs and weapons. Barlow and his companion were arrested.

In Barlow's motion for discovery under the *Armstrong* standard, he alleged that he had been "pursued, stopped, interviewed, and investigated by Drug Enforcement Administration agents based on his race." Barlow presented preliminary statistical evidence which indicated that African-American males were singled out for stops, whereas white males were not. He requested the names and races of all individuals stopped by the agents during a five-year period. In rejecting his motion, the court held that allegations of racial profiling are analyzed under the same standard of complaints of selective prosecution. The court stated that "Barlow needed to demonstrate that the agents' actions had a discriminatory effect and that the agents had a discriminatory purpose when they approached him." Without this evidence, Barlow could not meet the standard in *Armstrong* to obtain discovery on a claim of racial profiling.

African-American males continue to be victims of racial profiling, even with new safeguards developed by state and federal law enforcement organizations. The selective enforcement is based on stereotypical biases directed at African-Americans by law enforcement officials.

DOI: 10.1057/9781137408433.0005

Further remedies are needed to prohibit and punish law enforcement officers engaging in such discriminatory conduct. Unfortunately, African-American males lack the political clout to force Congress and other governmental officials to respond in a meaningful manner to prohibit the racial profiling of African-American males and other minorities. Moreover, the courts have failed to safeguard their constitutional rights to travel without fear of being stopped, searched, and arrested by law enforcement officials on the basis of their race and gender.

2.3   Racial disparities in sentencing of African-American males

Racial disparities in sentencing practices and policies of the criminal justice system also contribute to the disproportionate number of African-American males in jails and prisons.[119] A number of studies suggest that African-American defendants are more likely to be incarcerated and receive more severe penalties when the victims and the judge are white.[120] Even more shocking is a study conducted in 1990 by the Federal Judicial Center which reported that African-Americans received an average of 49% higher sentences than whites in cases involving drug trafficking with possession of a firearm.[121]

Approximately twenty years later, sentencing disparities still exist between African-American and white offenders. According to the Department of Justice, for the period October 1, 2009, and September 30, 2010, the average number of months of incarceration for drug offenses for African-Americans was 104.8, whereas for whites it was 68.1. There is even a wider disparity when considering all offenses.[122]

A 2013 study by the American Civil Liberties Union on Marijuana arrests between 2001 and 2010 determined:

> A Black person is 3.73 times more likely to be arrested for marijuana possession than a White person, even though Blacks and Whites use marijuana at similar rates. Such racial disparities in marijuana possession arrests exist in all regions of the country, in counties large and small, urban and rural, wealthy and poor, and with large and small Black populations. Indeed, in over 96% of counties with more than 30,000 people in which at least 2% of the residents are Black, Blacks are arrested at higher rates than Whites for marijuana possession.[123]

It is quite evident from the multitude of studies and reports from both the federal and state governments, and research experts that African-American offenders continue to receive longer sentences than whites for similar offenses. The reason for these disparities must be shared equally with state and federal judges, prosecutors, and Congress. It will take a concerted effort on all stakeholders to end the disparity.

In 1984, Congress enacted the Sentencing Reform Act of 1984,[124] which established the United States Sentencing Commission ("Sentencing Commission").[125] The Sentencing Commission was delegated with authority to promulgate Sentencing Guidelines for federal courts.[126] In 1987, the Sentencing Commission promulgated the Federal Sentencing Guidelines ("Sentencing Guidelines"), in part, to eliminate racial disparity in sentencing. To accomplish this goal, most of the judges' discretion in sentencing was removed. In its place, the guidelines established minimum sentences for certain offenses.

Five years later, the U.S. General Accounting Office ("GAO") issued a report indicating that due to "data limitation...[it is] impossible to know how effective the Federal Sentencing Guidelines...have been in reducing racial and other disparities in the sentences given to similar offenders for similar crimes."[127] The GAO report, however, indicated that in some areas of the Sentencing Guidelines there were still disparities in sentencing between African-Americans and whites for the same offense.[128] Further, the GAO report suggested that the way prosecutors plea bargain with defendants may adversely impact African-Americans and interfered with the Sentencing Commission's mission of eliminating disparity based on race.[129]

In 1993, the Justice Department released a report which examined whether there were racial and ethnic disparities imposed on federal offenders before and after the guidelines became fully effective. The study found in part that:

> During 1986-1988, before full implementation of sentencing guidelines, white, black and Hispanic offenders received similar sentences, on average, in federal district courts.
>
> Among federal offenders sentenced under guidelines from January 20, 1989 to June 30, 1990, there were substantial aggregate differences in sentences imposed on white, black, and Hispanic offenders.
>
> During this period, 85% of Hispanic offenders and 78% of black offenders were sentenced to imprisonment, compared with 72% of white offenders.
>
> On average, black offenders sentenced to prison during this period had imposed sentences that were 41% longer than for whites (21 months longer).[130]

DOI: 10.1057/9781137408433.0005

An earlier report from the Sentencing Commission attempted to determine whether there was still disparity in sentencing by federal courts. This report indicated disparity was still present in certain offenses and eliminated in others. The report, however, failed to squarely address the issue of racial disparities. Twenty years later, a review of the Sentencing Commission's 2012 *Sourcebook of Federal Sentencing Statistics* indicates that 82.6 crack cocaine defendants were black and 6.7 were white. Clearly, if sentences are longer for crack offenses, African-American males will be negatively impacted.[131]

A number of states have researched whether there were racial disparities in state court sentencing. For example, the Minnesota Sentencing Guideline Commission reported that during the 1980s, the number of blacks arrested for narcotics rose by 500%, while the arrest rate for whites for the same offenses rose 30%.[132] This disparity in arrest rates between blacks and whites correlated to a disparity between sentences given to blacks and whites by the courts. The Minnesota Commission also reported the following number of offenders sentenced for felony convictions: "Between 1981 and 1991, the number of cases increased 42% for whites; 53% for American Indians; 204% for African-Americans; and 388% for other races. Over half of the increase for African-Americans has occurred since 1987."[133]. Years later, there is evidence that African-Americans are still disproportionally sentenced based on the type of drug charges in Minnesota,[134] as well as in other state correctional systems.

There have been a number of constitutional challenges in court to various provisions of the Sentencing Guidelines, particularly the provision which requires a much stiffer penalty for crack cocaine versus powder cocaine.[135] More African-Americans are charged with possession of crack cocaine than powder cocaine.[136] This leads to African-Americans being incarcerated more often and receiving greater penalties. In *United States v. Majied*,[137] a federal district court deviated from the Sentencing Guidelines because young African-American males were disproportionately impacted by the requirement that they receive a harsher sentence for distribution and possession of crack cocaine. On appeal, the Eighth Circuit vacated the lower court's decision to impose a lesser sentence than was mandated by the Sentencing Guidelines.[138] Even though the courts recognized that African-Americans are disproportionately impacted by the Federal Sentencing Guidelines, they nevertheless refused to find any provision of the statute unconstitutional.[139]

DOI: 10.1057/9781137408433.0005

The U.S. Sentencing Commission recommended to Congress changes to the Sentencing Guidelines on the usage of crack and cocaine, which would have a lesser discriminatory impact on African-Americans.[140] However, Congress failed to take any meaningful actions. Congress was well aware of the disproportionate impact the statute had on and continues to have on African-American males; yet, Congress sat idly by and allowed thousands of African-American males to be charged under this race-based statute.

It is widely known and accepted that African-American male offenders are disproportionately impacted by the Federal Sentencing Guidelines. For example, in 2002, African-Americans received approximately 25% of sentences issued by U.S. District Courts under the U.S. Sentencing Commission Guidelines.[141] Since the Federal Sentencing Reform Act was promulgated in 1984, to limit probation in the Federal system, offenders have been required to serve longer sentences. Even with state laws which attempt to have consistency in sentencing regardless of race, African-American offenders still serve more time than whites for violent and rape offenses in state prisons.[142]

Under the Sentencing Guidelines African-Americans receive longer and more severe penalties for the use and sale of crack cocaine, whereas whites who are charged with the use and sale of cocaine receive less time in prison. Indeed, whites who are arrested and charged with cocaine may be able to receive rehabilitation provided by their health care provider in lieu of incarceration. Similarly, after the Civil War, the newly freed slave received more severe penalties than whites who committed the same or similar criminal acts. A prime example of disparity was in cases involving the stealing of a hog or chicken by a black slave versus a white offender. Historian Pau Finkelman described the disparity in a Virginia law against stealing hogs, which:

> [P]rovided a penalty of twenty-five lashes on a bare back or a ten pound fine for white offenders while non-whites, would receive thirty-nine lashes, with no chance of paying a fine to avoid the whipping.[143]

Finally, in 2005, the Supreme Court in *United States v. Booker*[144] held that the Guidelines were "effectively advisory" not mandatory. This again opened the door for federal judges more discretion in sentencing. A light at the end of a long nightmare of locking up African-American males was slowly coming to end.

DOI: 10.1057/9781137408433.0005

In 2010, Congress passed the Fair Sentencing Act which finally reduced the sentencing disparity between the races. In place of a 100 to 1 ratio between crack and cocaine, Congress agreed on a compromise of 18 to 1. In *Dorsey v. U.S.*,[145] the Supreme Court acknowledged that the Act had been passed, in part, because "the public had come to understand sentences embodying the 100 to 1 ratio as reflecting unjustified race-based differences."[146] This was a major decision by Congress but the disparities still exist because of this differential between the two drugs. In March 2014, Attorney General Eric Holder testified before the Sentencing Commission and proposed that the Federal Sentencing Guidelines be used primarily for the "most serious drug traffickers."[147] If approved, the number of inmates would decrease, thus releasing thousands of young African-American males who were incarcerated for low-level trafficking crimes.

Even more disheartening is the fact that the new Sentencing Guidelines are not applied retroactively; thus, thousands of African-American males may remain incarcerated, some for life because of the early sentencing law, which had a discriminatory impact on African-Americans. The Sentencing Commission reports that 80% of federal prisoners charged under the previous Act are African-American males. In *U.S. v. Blewett*[148] the court stated that:

> Yet, despite the passage of the Act and the Supreme Court's condemnation of the 100–to–1 ratio more than 17,000 such crack prisoners sentenced under the old, racially discriminatory law are not eligible for resentencing.[149]

The failure to not make the Guidelines and the new statute retroactive illustrates how, once again, African-American males are treated adversely in the justice system. Hopefully, the Congress will not wait another twenty years to end all disparity in federal sentencing laws.[150]

2.4   Racial disparities in prosecutorial decisions

The Sentencing Guidelines were promulgated primarily to eliminate discriminatory practices in sentencing individuals after trial. However, before there is a criminal trial and ultimately sentencing, individuals must first be charged with a crime. This responsibility rests with state and federal prosecutors. The Sentencing Guidelines have in effect moved the capacity for discrimination from judges to prosecutors. There were concerns that prosecutorial discretion and plea bargaining practices might "reintroduce unwarranted sentencing disparities into the criminal justice system."[151] These concerns, as will be shown, are amply justified.

The prosecutor has broad discretion to determine what crime the defendant will be charged with, if charged at all.[152] Of course, a lesser charge normally results in a lesser penalty—that is, a lesser jail term. The prosecutor also has unbridled authority to plea bargain a case allowing the defendant(s) to admit to a lesser offense and avoid trial in lieu of a more severe charge with a trial.[153] How this presentencing process impacts African-Americans has been the topic of a number of studies.[154]

One leading statistical study conducted to determine whether the race of the victim was a factor prosecutors considered when determining whether to proceed with the severest charge available under the law revealed that when the victim was white, prosecutors were more likely to seek full prosecution.[155] Indeed, in high-profile cases where the defendant is black, the prosecutor may be more likely to pursue the greatest penalty; this often involves the death penalty in homicide cases where the victim is white.[156] A study of homicide defendants in Florida further supports the thesis that prosecutorial decisions are often impacted by racial bias.[157] Even the U.S. Supreme Court reports that a study of the death penalty determined that prosecutors sought the death penalty in 70% of the cases involving black defendants and white victims; 15% of cases involving black defendants and black victims; and 19% of the cases involving white defendants and black victims. The Supreme Court, nevertheless, ruled against the defendant who alleged the death penalty system was racial bias.[158] The Courts' acceptance of such discriminatory conduct on the part of prosecutors sanctions the use of disparate treatment at other stages of the criminal justice system. It also supports the argument that the justice system values the lives of whites more than the lives of African-American males. Such unconscionable decisions by the prosecutors should violate the Equal Protection Clause, if the prosecutors' decisions were racially motivated.

In an effort to reduce the potential risk of racial disparity in how prosecutors use discretion in making prosecutorial decisions, the Vera's Prosecution and Racial Justice Program was created.[159] The program is a nationwide initiative, working with prosecutors, to collect and analyze data from specific prosecutors' offices to determine whether there is any evidence of racial disparity.[160] Clearly, determining whether discretionary decisions on who to charge and what to plea bargaining will bring to

DOI: 10.1057/9781137408433.0005

light any racial disparity, particularly involving African-American male defendants who are disproportionately prosecuted.[161]

In another study investigating whether prosecutors are more likely to reject felony charges initiated against blacks, whites, and Hispanics, the results indicated that disparity existed against blacks and Hispanics.[162] Various other studies support this finding of a disparity between whites and blacks as to when charges are filed and pursued by prosecutors.[163]

Aside from the issue of prosecutorial discretion, the racial makeup of the prosecutor's office may also impact how charges are pursued against African-American defendants. The typical prosecutor's office is predominately staffed by young white male attorneys.[164] The power of prosecutorial discretion is wielded "almost exclusively [by] the hands of white males."[165] State prosecutors are elected officials. Thus, they have the continuous burden of illustrating to the public that they are "tough on crime" in order to get re-elected. Prosecuting low-level drug dealers in the African-American community gives prosecutors immediate news coverage. A similar scenario is found at the federal level.[166]

A lack of representation of African-Americans in the prosecutor's office gives the appearance of, and likely leads to, a lack of sensitivity to the needs of the African-American community. A combination of racial disparity in how African-American males are charged and prosecuted, along with racial bias in the sentencing laws, has resulted in mass numbers of African-American males being incarcerated.

2.5   Law enforcement and police brutality

In the early hours of March 3, 1991, Rodney King, a black man in Los Angeles, was severely beaten and brutalized by police officers.[167] Furthermore, their conduct was videotaped and repeatedly viewed by the public on national television. Many Americans were pathetically mystified that such conduct occurred as if the videotape had captured South African policemen beating a black man in South Africa.[168]

Many Americans still have not fully acknowledged that a vicious crime was committed or that Rodney King's civil rights were violated. The sentiment of many is that if King would have "just laid still" through the beating, his injuries would not have been as severe.[169] For African-Americans, however, the Rodney King beating was not out of the ordinary, but reflects the general treatment that African-Americans, particularly males, have received from police departments. The only difference between the Rodney King incident and many other incidents of police brutality involving black males is that the officers' conduct was videotaped and continuously aired on national television.

Before the court could resolve the Rodney King incident, the nation was again stunned by another violent act directed at an African-American male motorist, Malice Greene, by white police officers in Detroit. Unlike the King situation, the beating of Malice Green was not videotaped. A black officer was at the scene but did not intervene, and the death of Malice Green was the end result.[170] According to witnesses, Malice Green, a 35-year-old African-American male, was stopped, beaten with a heavy flashlight, and kicked by two police officers, while at least five other officers watched. Green subsequently died of head injuries in the hospital. The officers insisted that Green resisted arrest.[171]

Cities, such as Los Angeles, Chicago, Denver, New York, Oakland, to name a few, have paid millions of dollars in damages for cases of police brutality against African-American males. For example, approximately one year before the Rodney King case, another police brutality case against the L.A.P.D. was decided when a jury awarded Joe Morgan, a black male and a member of the National Baseball Hall of Fame, $540,000 because the police used excessive force when they mistook him for a drug courier. It appeared that he was selectively stopped because he was a black male.[172] In Prince George's County, Maryland, a jury awarded $1.9 million against four policemen for violating the civil rights of a Ghanaian when he died as a result of "blunt force trauma" by the arresting officers.[173] In 1980, an African-American male insurance executive, Arthur McDuffie, was beaten to death by white Miami police officers; the officers were later acquitted of any charges.[174] In Columbus, Ohio, a white police officer was indicted on felonious assault charges for striking an African-American male in the mouth with a flashlight.[175] In 2004, the city of New York agreed to pay $3 million to the family of Amado Diallo, who was unarmed and killed by police in a hail of 41 bullets. Again, in 2010, the city of New York agreed to pay $7 million to the family of Sean Bell who was shot and killed in 2006 by police in a fury of 50 bullets directed at him.[176] The number of police brutality/misconduct cases filed against the City of Chicago is so plentiful that the city has proposed in 2014 to issue approximately 100 million dollars in bonds, some of which will be used to settle such cases.[177]

DOI: 10.1057/9781137408433.0005

Each time it is publicized that an African-American male has been brutally victimized there is an outcry from the public to end police brutality. A short time thereafter, the public concern is quickly forgotten and the Africa-American community retreat back to a passive position, until another tragic event occurs. There is presently no national or aggressive state plan of action designed to prevent or correct abusive police misconduct directed at African-American men. In addition, African-American communities have failed to formulate a cohesive response to police brutality.

2.6   Racial bias in the death penalty

More than 3,000 prisoners are on death row, and approximately 40% are African-Americans.[178] As of December 31, 2011, the total number of death row inmates recorded by the U.S. Department of Justice was 3,082. The race of inmates on death row was as follows:

White	55.3%
Black	41.8%
Latino/a	14%
Other	3.0%[179]

Since the death penalty was reinstated in 1976, of the 1,320 executed, 454 or 34.39% have been African-Americans. The race of inmates executed since capital punishment was reinstated in 1976 is as follows:

White	741 (56.14%)
Black	454 (34.39%)
Latino/a	102 (7.73%)
Native American	16 (1.21%)
Asian	7 (0.53%)[180]

African-Americans make up approximately 12% of the general population. Clearly, African-American males are disproportionately overrepresented on death row and subsequently executed. Study after study has substantiated that race is a significant factor in the decision to sentence a defendant to die, especially if the defendant is black and the victim is white.[181] A review of the defendant–victim racial combinations of those on death row reveals that 80, or 26.02%, involved a black defendant and a white-victim, while only one, or 0.33%, involved a white defendant and a black-victim. In 1991, the National Association for the Advancement

DOI: 10.1057/9781137408433.0005

of Colored People provided the following testimony regarding the death penalty before members of Congress:

> A 1981 study by Professor Rudelet of the University of Florida found that a "black on white homicide is 37.7 times more likely to get death."
>
> A 1983 study by Professor Bernard Bray, Talladega College, of capital murder cases in Alabama found that killers of whites are 10 times more likely to be tried for the death penalty and 8 times more likely to receive the death penalty than killers of blacks.
>
> In Illinois, killers of whites are 4 times more likely to be put to death than killers of blacks, according to the study of Gross and Mauro.[182]

Even the Supreme Court, in striking down the death penalty in Georgia more than twenty years ago, stated that "[t]he death penalty is disproportionately imposed and carried out on the poor, the Negro and the members of unpopular groups."[183] In *United States v. Wiley*, the Court stated, "[t]here has been an enormous danger of injustice when a black man accused of raping a white woman is tried before a white jury. Of the 455 men executed for rape since 1930, 405 (89%) were black. In the vast majority of these cases the complainant was white."[184] States with death penalty statutes rewrote them after 1977 to eliminate arbitrariness in capital penalty sentencing. These attempted remedies failed to address the issue of racial discrimination. Death row statistics for African-American males are higher in some states than the national average.

In 1987, the issue of racial disparity in death penalty sentencing was squarely before the Supreme Court, when Warren McCleskey, an African-American male, challenged his death sentence. In *McCleskey v. Kemp*,[185] the Supreme Court was presented with a thorough study which reviewed more than 2,500 cases of homicides in Georgia for a six-year period. The report validated what most people already knew—that race was a major factor in deciding who received the death penalty.[186] A summary of the report by the American Civil Liberties Union states:

> Death was imposed in 34% of the white-victim cases but in only 14% of similarly aggravated black-victim cases.
>
> The odds of receiving a death sentence in a white-victim case was 4.3 times greater than the odds of receiving a death sentence in a comparable black-victim case.
>
> Nearly six of every 10 defendants who were sentenced to death for killing white victims would not have been sentenced to death had their victims been black.

DOI: 10.1057/9781137408433.0005

Nearly 90% of those executed since 1977 were convicted of murdering whites, while in the same period, almost half of the homicide victims were black.

In the same period of time, all seven of the persons executed in Georgia were convicted of killing whites. Six of the seven executed were black.[187]

Even though the Supreme Court did not dispute that the study was correct in finding race to be a factor in death sentences, the Court refused to grant McCleskey relief unless he could prove that he personally was a victim of intentional discrimination.[188] The Supreme Court stated, "McCleskey's arguments are best presented to the legislative bodies." The Court further stated, "It is not the responsibility, or indeed even the right, of this court to determine the appropriate punishment for particular crimes." Interestingly, in *Callins v. Collins*,[189] Justice Blackmun announced he would no longer support the use of the death penalty, in part because of the study presented in *McCleskey* that showed racism was a factor in determining whether an individual would receive the death penalty.[190]

Unfortunately, Congress has failed to adequately address the issue of racial disparity in death penalty sentencing. While Congress "gridlocked," McCleskey was executed in 1991 with no relief, other than the cold embrace of death. The race of the defendant and victim continue to be factors in death penalty cases.[191]

In 1988, Congress passed the Anti-Drug Abuse Act which directed the GAO to "report to the Congress on whether or not any or all of the various [sentencing] procedures create a significant risk that the race of a defendant, or the race of a victim...influence the likelihood that defendants...will be sentenced to death."[192]

In response to Congress's directive, the GAO analyzed 28 studies to determine whether race was a factor in death penalty sentencing. In summarizing their conclusions, the GAO made the following findings:

> Our synthesis of the 28 studies shows a pattern of evidence indicating racial disparities in the charging, sentencing, and imposition of the death penalty after the Furman decision.
>
> In 82 percent of the studies, race of victim was found to influence the likelihood of being charged with capital murder or receiving the death penalty, i.e., those who murdered whites were found to be more likely to be sentenced to death than those who murdered blacks.
>
> The race of victim influence was found at all stages of the criminal justice system process, although there were variations among studies as to whether

there was a race of victim influence at specific stages. The evidence for the race of victim influence was stronger for the earlier stages of the justice process (e.g., prosecutorial decision to charge defendant with a capital offense, decision to proceed to trial rather than plea bargain) than in later stages.

Finally, more than three-fourths of the studies that identified a race of defendant effect found that black defendants were more likely to receive the death penalty.

To summarize, the synthesis supports a strong race of victim influence. The race of offender influence is not as clear cut and varies across a number of dimensions. Although there are limitations to the studies' methodologies, they are of sufficient quality to support the synthesis findings.[193]

Both Houses of Congress have conducted hearings on the issue of racism in death penalty to support passage of a federal law that would prohibit racially discriminatory capital sentencing.[194] During the House Subcommittee hearing, the Death Penalty Information Center released a study of the Chattahoochee Judicial District of Georgia which shows that blacks typically received harsher sentencing, and that the death penalty was sought more often when the victim was white than when the victim was black.[195] However, after much protracted testimony and statistical data which supported allegations that African-American males are systematically discriminated against in receiving the death penalty, Congress failed to pass legislation to provide relief.

Unlike Congress, a number of states have moved forward with addressing the disparity in the death penalty cases. In 2009, the state of North Carolina took the unprecedented step and passed the Racial Justice Act.[196] The Act prohibited the use of race in death penalty cases. Specifically, the Act stated that "no person shall be subjected to or given a sentence of death or shall be executed pursuant to any judgment that was sought or obtained on the basis of race."[197] Surprisingly, in 2012 a North Carolina superior court judge held in *North Carolina v. Robinson*[198] that race was a significant factor in a death sentence. The judge relied in part on a study conducted by the Michigan State University which found that race was a significant factor in jury selection in capital proceeding in North Carolina.[199] Marcus Robinson, an African-American male, sentence was changed to life in prison. Judge Weeks stated that:

> Discrimination in jury selection frustrates the commitment of African-Americans to full participation in civic life. One of the stereotypes particularly offensive to African–American citizens is that they are not interested in seeing criminals brought to justice. African-Americans who have been

excluded from jury service on account of race compare their experiences to the injustice and humiliations of the Jim Crow era.[200]

This victory to end racial disparity in the death penalty cases in North Carolina was short-lived. In summer of 2013, the North Carolina legislature moved quickly to repeal the Racial Justice Act. Other states such as Connecticut, California, and New Hampshire have made efforts to end disparity in death penalty. Because the death penalty is still used by a number of states, African-American males continue to face a system where there is an overwhelming amount of scientific data to conclude the death penalty system is discriminatory.[201] Thus, the death penalty remains the "first cousin to lynching" of African-American males.[202]

2.7   Racial disparities in the juvenile justice system

African-American youth, particularly males, are clearly "at risk" of becoming prisoners in the juvenile justice system.[203] As with the adult prisoners, young African-American males have become casualties of the "war on drugs." They too are disproportionately arrested, detained, and prosecuted.[204] For example, in 2011, the Justice Department reported that

▸ Black Youth were overrepresented in juvenile arrests.
▸ More than half (51%) of all juvenile arrest for violent crimes involved black youth.
▸ 17% juvenile arrests were black youth, between the ages of 10–17.[205]

The confinement of African-American male youth in state correction facilities parallels the staggering number of adult African-American males in prison.[206] Similarly, African-American male youths in the juvenile justice system are treated less favorably than white male youths. A study on racial bias in the State of Florida juvenile justice system revealed that African-American youths "were more likely to be recommended for formal processing, referred to court, adjudicated delinquent, and given harsher disposition than comparable white offenders."[207] The Florida Study also revealed that "[t]he differential treatment of minority juveniles results, at least in part, from racial and ethnic bias on the part of enough individual police officers, intake workers, prosecutors, and judges, to make the system operate as if it intended to discriminate against minorities."

DOI: 10.1057/9781137408433.0005

Twenty years after the above study on Florida's juvenile system, there is still evidence of disparity. In 2011, a study released by the Florida Department of Juvenile Justice on delinquency referred from Florida schools revealed that African-American youth, particularly males, are at risk of being referred from school to the juvenile system. The study stated in part:

▸ While only representing 21% of the youth ages 10–17 in Florida, black males and females accounted for almost half (46%) of all school-related referrals.

▸ [B]lack males were substantially more likely to receive commitment dispositions or to have their cases transferred to adult court.[208]

These numbers suggest that African-American males are on track to move from a school environment to a correctional system. At a young age, African-American males will be arrested by "police officers and sheriff's deputies" for acts of alleged delinquency in school. This type of treatment of African-American youth is not unique to Florida; it is an everyday occurrence around the country. Unfortunately, African-American males who are removed from school and placed in the juvenile system are destined to drop out of school. This is not to suggest that an African-American male youth should never be placed in the juvenile system. The problem is that Africa-American males are disproportionally placed in the judicial system as the first response to an issue in school, and not the last resort. School systems must develop other alternatives to removing African-American males from school as a quick fix to addressing their educational challenges. They are often faced with family and bullying challenges that impact their behavior and performance at school.[209] Instead of automatically referring them to the juvenile system, consider referring them to the school psychologist or counselor.

When African-American male youths are released from confinement and returned to school, they are often labeled as troubled black males; therefore, they are isolated and segregated from other students. This will negatively impact their self-esteem and motivation to remain in school. This may cause them to engage in disruptive behavior to get attention that the "smart" students and athletics appear to be receiving. They will again be referred back to the juvenile system without a resolution of the kind or type of educational services they need and deserve to be success-ful in school.

DOI: 10.1057/9781137408433.0005

A disproportionate number of African-American male youths are transferred to adult courts, where the penalties are much more severe.[210] A study by the Juvenile Justice Initiative of children in Cook County, Illinois, who are referred to adult court, determined that:

> Racial disparities are much more profound in Illinois, African-Americans represent 44 percent of the youth population in Cook County, but from 2000 to 2002, 99 percent of children automatically transferred to adult court were African-American or Latino.[211]

Juveniles who are remanded to the adult criminal justice system are typically viewed by prosecutors and the courts as not viable candidates for rehabilitation. Prosecutors have discretion to proceed with a case in juvenile or criminal court. Too often, African-American males who are poor, uneducated, and raised by a single-parent are waived over to adult court. Even though there are issues in the juvenile system, young African-American males have a better chance of becoming responsible young men than if they are placed in an adult system at a young age.

The National Council on Crime & Delinquency reports that research has determined that to reduce the automatic flow of African-American youth from juvenile to adult court, states must review and modify their transfer statutes to limit the criteria for transfers.[212] A failure to do so will result in African-American youth being disproportionately transferred to adult facilities where they will less likely get counseling and educational support.

Because the educational system has failed to educate and develop young African-American males, they are destined to enter the prison pipeline. As a result of the high rates of suspensions, exclusions, and dropouts of African-American males in school, they will ultimately find their way to the correctional system. Action for Children defined the school-to-prison pipeline in this manner:

> Underfunded schools, harsh discipline practices, school policing, and lack of appropriate alternative education options are the segments of the school-to-prison pipeline that can move vulnerable students towards the juvenile or adult criminal system.[213]

A failed educational system will guide more young African-American males from school to the juvenile court system and ultimately the adult court system. In 2012, the Justice Department sued the City of Meridian, Mississippi, for operating a "school to prison system." Specifically, the complaint alleged, in part that:

DOI: 10.1057/9781137408433.0005

[t]he defendants help to operate a school-to-prison pipeline in which the rights of children in Meridian are repeatedly and routinely violated. As a result, children in Meridian have been systematically incarcerated for allegedly committing minor offenses, including school disciplinary infractions, and are punished disproportionately without due process of law. The students most affected by this system are African-American children and children with disabilities.[214]

The parties reached a settlement of the case in 2013. The settlement should protect African-American students, especially males, from being suspended, expelled, and arrested at school in violation of their constitution rights. Hopefully, this highly publicized litigation will encourage other school districts and state juvenile justice systems to review and modify their systems in a manner to end discriminatory practice. More importantly, schools and courts must develop alternatively to just suspending and locking up young African-American males.

Notes

1   *The Sentencing Project, Report of the Sentencing Project to the United Nations Human Rights Committee; Regarding Racial Disparities in the United States Criminal Justice System* (2013), *available at* http://sentencingproject.org/doc/publications/rd_ICCPR%20Race%20and%20Justice%20Shadow%20Report.pdf.

2   *United Nations Office on Drugs and Crime, International Statistics and Crime and Justice* 164–165 (2010), *available at* https://www.unodc.org/unodc/en/data-and-analysis/crimedata.htm.

3   *Pew Charitable Trusts, Collateral Costs: Incarceration's Effect on Economic Mobility* 6 (2010), *available at* http://www.pewtrusts.org/news_room_detail.aspx?id=60964.

4   *U.S. Dep't of Justice, Bureau of Statistics, Prisoners in 2012*, at 25 (December 2013), *available at* http://www.bjs.gov/content/pub/press/p12acpr.cfm.

5   *U.S. Dep't of Justice, Bureau of Statistics. Correctional Populations in the United States, 2012* (December 2013), *available at* http://www.bjs.gov/content/pub/pdf/cpus12.pdf.

6   For a discussion of the growth of prisons, *see Prison Policy Initiative, Incarceration Rates Growth Causes*, http://www.urban.org/UploadedPDF/412693-The-Growth-and-Increasing-Cost-of-the-Federal-Prison-System.pdf. Provides a list of data bases on research related to incarceration and prisons (last visited May 29, 2014); Nancy La Vigne & Julie Samuels, *Urban Institute, the Growth & Increasing Cost of the Federal Prison*

DOI: 10.1057/9781137408433.0005

System: Drivers and Potential Solutions (December 2012), *available at* http://www.urban.org/UploadedPDF/412693-The-Growth-and-Increasing-Cost-of-the-Federal-Prison-System.pdf; G. Pascal Zachary, Economists Say Prison Boom Will Take Toll, WALL ST. J., September 29, 1995.

7   Dorothy Roberts, *The Social and Moral Cost of Mass Incarceration in African Communities*, 56 Stan. L. Rev. 1271, 1279 (2004); Farai Chideya et al., *Endangered Family, Newsweek*, August 30, 1993, at 16, 25; Damon J. Keith, Symposium, *200 Years of the Penitentiary: Criminal, Social and Economic Justice*, 34 How. L.J. 483, 528–533 (1991) (surveying the impact of incarceration of African-American males on African-American communities and families, e.g., single-parent households, lack of mentors, poverty, and welfare).

8   See, Dorothy E. Roberts, *Criminal Justice and Black Families: The Collateral Damages of Over-Enforcement*, 34 U.C. Davis L. Rev. 1005 (Summer 2001).

9   *Sentencing Project Report of the United Nation Human Rights Committee, Regarding Racial Disparities in the United States Criminal Justice System*, August 2013, p. 1, citing Marc Mauer, *Addressing Racial Disparities in Incarceration*, 91 Supp. 3. The Prison J. 875, 885 (September 2011).

10   *See generally* Laura T. Sweeney & Craig Haney, *The Influence of Race on Sentencing: A Meta-Analytic Review of Experimental Studies*, 10 Behav. Sci. & L. 179 (1992); Joan Petersilia, *Racial Disparities in the Criminal Justice System: A Summary*, 31 Crime & Delinq. 15 (1985); Patrick A. Langan, *Racism on Trial: New Evidence to Explain the Racial Composition of Prisoners in the United States*, 76 J. Crim. L. & Criminology 666 (1985); Norval Morris, *Race and Crime: What Evidence Is There That Race Influences Results in the Criminal Justice System?*, 72 Judicature 111 (1988); Adjoa A. Aiyetoro, *The Criminal Justice System: Racism and Genocide*, Nba Mag., March 1989, at 14.

11   *Preliminary Report on Race and Washington's Criminal Justice System, Seattle U. L. Rev.*, 35, 623, 626 (2012).

12   *Id.* at 628.

13   John Pawasarat & Lois M. Quinn, *Wisconsin's Mass Incarceration of African-American Males: Workforce Challenges* (2013), *available at* ps://www4.uwm.edu/eti/2013/BlackImprisonment.pdf.

14   Vincent Schiraldi & Ziedenberg, *Justice Policy Institute, Race and Incarceration in Maryland*, 5 (October 23, 2003) *available a*t www.justicepolicy.org/research/2029.

15   *Id. at* 9.

16   Hearing Before the Subcommittee on Crime, Terrorism, and Homeland security of the Committee on the Judiciary House of Representatives, One Hundred Eleventh Congress, First Session, *Racial Disparities in the Criminal Justice System*, October 29, 2009.

17   *U.S. Dep't of Justice, Bureau of Statistics, Prisoners in 2012*, at 25 (December 2013), *available at* http://www.bjs.gov/content/pub/press/p12acpr.cfm.

DOI: 10.1057/9781137408433.0005

18   *Id. at* 37.

19   *Id.*

20   *See,* Marc Mauer, *Sentencing Project, Intended and Unintended Consequences: State Racial Disparities in Imprisonment* (January 1997), *available at* www. sentencingproject.org/ (last visited May 28, 2014).

21   *U.S. Dep't of Justice, Bureau of Justice Statistics, Prisoners in 2011,* at 7 (December 2012), *available at* http://www.bjs.gov/index.cfm?ty=pbdetail&iid=4559.

22   Graham Boyd, *American Civil Liberties Union, the Drug War is the New Jim Crow,* July 31, 2001, *available at* https://www.aclu.org/print/drug-lawreform/ drug-war-new-jim-crow.

23   *Id.*

24   *Justice Policy Institute, Cellblock or Classrooms, the Funding of Higher Education and Corrections and its Impact on African-American Males, available at* http:// www.justicepolicy.org/cocl/core.htm. There has been some disagreement among researchers whether this statement is correct. It appears that a review of a number of African-American males under the various state and federal systems may exceed the number of African-American males in college.

25   *Pew Research Social & Demographic Trends, King's Dream Remains an Elusive Goal: Many Americans see Racial Disparities* (2013), *available at* http//www. pewsocialtrends.org/2013/08/22kings-dream-remains-an-elusive-goal-many-american-see-racial-disparities/4/#incarceration-rate.

26   *Sentencing Project, The Expanding Federal Prison Population; The Federal Prison Population: A Statistical Analysis, available at* www.sentencingproject.org/ (last visited May 28, 2014).

27   *Bureau of Justice Statistics, Correctional 2012 supra note 5, at 10.*

28   *Federal Bureau of Prisons, Inmate Race, available at* http://www.bop.gov/about/ statistics/statistics-inmate-race.jsp (Reports indicate that as of January 25, 2014, 76,961 or 37.1% of the inmates were black and 123,457 or 59.5% of the inmates were white.) The Sentencing Project reports that "Two-thirds (68% of Federal Prisoners are Racial and Ethnic Minorities—39% Black, 29% Latino." The SENTENCING PROJECT, *The Expanding Federal Prison Population, supra* note 26; Alfred Blumstein, *Racial Disproportional of U.S. Prison Population Revisited,* 64 U. COLO. L. REV. 760, 773 (1993).

29   *See,* Pamela E. Oliver, *Racial Disparities in Imprisonment: Some Basic Information* (2001), *available at* http://www.ssc.wisc.edu/~oliver/racial/ oliver%20focus%202001.pdf.

30   *Bureau of Justice Statistics, Correctional 2012 supra note 5, at 10.*

31   *Bureau of Justice Statistics, Prisoners 2011 supra note 21, at 23.*

32   *New Orleans: Prisoners Abandoned To Flood Waters, Human Rights Watch, available at* http://www.hrw.org/english/documents/2005/09/22/usdom11773. htm (last visited May 28, 2014).

33   Jordan Flaherty and Tamika Middleton, *Imprisoned in New Orleans, Color Lines, available at* http:www.arc.org/C-Lines/CLARchive/Story 9-1-06.html

DOI: 10.1057/9781137408433.0005

(Describes how 7,000 prisoners were treated after Hurricane Katrina) (last visited May 28, 2014).

34   *Louisiana State Penitentiary, General, available at* http://www.corections. state.a.us./lse/general.htm (last visited May 28, 2014).

35   *Id.*

36   David Walsh, *Life in Prison, available at* http://www.wsns.org/arts/1998/ may1998/farm-323.html (last visited May 28, 2014).

37   *Introduction: The Louisiana State Penitentiary at Angola, available at* http:// prisonactivist.org/Angola/history/.shtml (last visited May 28, 2014),

38   *History of Angola, available at* http://www.corrections.state./a.us/isp/history. htm (providing more information about the Farm).

39   Kevin J. Strom, *Bureau of Justice Statistics, Profile of State Prisoners Under the Age 18, 1985–1997 – Special Report* (February 2000), *available at* http://www.bjs. gov/index.cfm?ty=pbdetail&iid=1121.

40   Ashley Gilpin, *The Impact of Mandatory Minimums and Truth-In Sentencing Laws and Their Relation to English Sentencing Policies*, 29 *Ariz. J. of Int'l & Comp.L.* 91 (2012): William J. Sabol et al., *Urban Institute Justice Policy Center, the Influences of Truth-in-Sentencing Reforms on Changes in States' Sentencing Practices and Prison Populations* (2002), *available at* www.urban.org/ UploadedPDF/410470_FINALTISrpt.pd; Paula M. Ditton & Doris James Wilson, *Bureau of Justice Statistics, Truth-in-Sentencing in State Prison Special Report* (January 1999), *available at* http://www.bjs.gov/content/pub/pdf/ tssp.pdf; also see, *Office of Justice Programs, Violent Offender Incarceration and Truth-in-Sentencing Incentive Grants: Program Guidance and Application Kit,* FY 1998, NCJ 168942 (1998); *Truth in Sentencing in State Prisons, BJS, Special Report,* NCJ 170032, February 1998.

41   *See, 42 U.S.C. Sec.* 13701–13713 (2000 & Supp. 2006); *U.S. Department of Justice, Fact Sheet, Violent Crime Control and Law Enforcement Act of 1994, available at* https://www.ncjrs.gov/txtfiles/billfs.txt.

42   Douglas A. McVay, *Race, Prisons and The Drug Laws, Common Sense for Drug Policy,* http://www.csdp.org (last visited May 28,2014).

43   Vincent Schivaldi, Jason Colburn, & Eric Lotke, *Justice Policy Institute, An Examination of the Impact of 3-Strike Laws, 10 Years After Their Enactment, available at* http://www.justicepolicy.org/uploads/justicepolicy/ documents/04-09_rep_threestrikesnatl_ac.pdf.pdf.

44   *Id., See also,* Marc Mauer, *Race to Incarcerate* (2006), *available at* (http://www. sentencingproject.org/detail/publication.cfm?publication_id=2 (Discusses whether the mass incarceration of individuals and the war on drugs has had any impact on reducing crime in America).

45   *See, Legislative Analyst's Office, a Primer: Three Strikes—the Impact after More Than a Decade* (October 2005) *available at* http://www.lao.ca.gov/2005/3_ strikes/3_strikes_102005.htm.

DOI: 10.1057/9781137408433.0005

46   Bureau of Justice Statistics, Prisoners 2011 supra note 21, at 43.

47   See State of California Corrections and Rehabilitation, Adult Population Projection, 2006–2011 (Spring 2006), available at www.cdcr.ca.gov/.

48   See, Brown v. Plata, 131 S. Ct. 1910 (2011); For a discussion of California's plan to reduce its population, see Bureau of Justice Statistics, Prisoners 2011, supra note 21, at 7.

49   Bureau of Justice Statistics, Correctional 2012 supra note 5, at 10.

50   U.S. Dep't of Justice, Bureau of Statistics, Jail Inmates at Midyear 2012-Statistical Table at 6 (May 2013), available at www.bjs.gov/.

51   Id. at 4.

52   Bureau of Justice Statistics, Prisoners 2011, supra note 21, at 13.

53   Id.

54   Lauren E. Glaze and Seri Palla, U.S. Dep't of Justice, Bureau of Statistics, Probations and Parole in the United States, 2004 at 1 (November 2005), available at www.bjs.gov/index.cfm?ty=pbdetail&iid=1108.

55   Id. at 2.

56   Id. at 6.

57   See, Paul Krugman, Prisons, Privatization, Patronage, N.Y. Times, June 21, 2012, available at http://www.nytimes.com/2012/06/22/opinion/krugman-prisons-privatization-patronage.html; Phil Smith, Private Prisons: Profit of Crime, Covert Action Quarterly (Fall 1993), available at http:://mediafilter.org./chq/pris (the correction budgets of local, state, and federal governments exceeded $20 billion dollars a year in 1990).

58   See, Kenneth M. Stampp, Southern Negro Slavery: To Make Them Stand in Fear, in American Negro Slavery 51–73 (Allen Weinstein and Frank Otto Gatell eds., 1979) (tactics used by slave owners to punish and control slaves, including having private jails).

59   U.S. Dep't of Justice, Bureau of Statistics, Prisoners in 2010, at 30 (2012), available at www.bjs.gov/index.cfm?ty=pbdetail&iid=2230.

60   Bureau of Statistics, Prisoners in 2012, supra note 4, at appendix.

61   Peter J. Duitsman, The Private Prison Experiment: A Private Sector Solution to Prison Overcrowding, 76 N.C.L. Rev. 2209 (1998); Charles H. Logan, Well Kept: Comparing Quality of Confinement in Private and Public Prisons, 83 J. Crim. L. & Criminology 577 (1992).

62   Allison Campbell, Cells For Sale: Prison Privatization and Human Rights, The Human Rights Debate, available at http://www.hrica/tribune/view/article.asp?ID=2640

63   Sourcebook of Criminal Justice Statistics, 99 (2003), available at https://www.ncjrs.gov/.../208.

64   Marc Mauer, Invisible Punishment, Block Housing Education, Voting. FOCUS, Joint Center For Political and Economic Studies (May/June 2003), available at www.sentencingproject.org/doc/publications/cc_mauer-focus.pdf.

DOI: 10.1057/9781137408433.0005

65   *See,* Stephen Hartnett, *Prison Labor, Slavery & Capitalism in Historical Perspective, available at* http://www.historyisaweapon.com/defcon1/hisprislacap.html (Describes the development of leased prison labor and the development of the "Correctional-Industrial Complex")

66   *Sourcebook, super* note 63 at 94.

67   *Sourcebook, super* note 63 at 99.

68   *U.S. Justice Department, Bureau of Labor Statistics Occupational Employment Statistics* (May 2013), *available at* http//www.bls.gov/oes/CURRENT/oes333012.htm.

69   David A. Harris, *ACLU, Driving While Black: Racial Profiling On Our Nation's Highways* (June 7, 1999), *available* at https://www.aclu.org/racial-justice/driving-while-black-racial-profiling-our-nations-highways.

70   98 F.3d 1181 (9th Cir. 1996).

71   *Id.* at 1191.

72   Tracey Maclin, *Justice Thurgood Marshall: Taking the Fourth Amendment Seriously,* 77 Cornell L. Rev. 723, 723 (1992).

73   *Price v. Kramer,* 200F.3d 1237, 1256 (9th Cir. 2003).

74   392 U.S. 1 (1968).

75   *Terry,* 392 U.S. at 27.

76   239 F. Supp. 2d 173 (D.R.I. 2003).

77   359 F.3d 24 (2004).

78   98 F.3d 118, 1187 (1996).

79   .734 A.2d 350 (N.J. Super. Ct. 1996).

80   *Id.* at 356.

81   Robin S. Engel, Jennifer Calnon Cherkauskas, & Michael R. Smith, *University of Cincinnati Policing Institute, Traffic Stop Data Analysis Study: Year 2 Final Report Xii* (November 20, 2008), *available at* www.azdps.gov/about/reports/docs/Traffic_Stop_Data_Report_2008.pdf.

82   Frank R. Baumgarter and Derek Epp, *Department of Political Science, University of North Carolina at Chapel Hill, North Carolina Traffic Stop Statistics Analysis 5* (February 1, 2012), *available at* http://www.newsobserver.com/2013/09/29/3238448/traffic-stop-numbers-show-racial.html.

83   Jack Mcdevitt, Janice Iwama and Lisa Bailey, *Institute on Race and Justice, Northeastern University Rhode Island Traffic Stop Statistics, Date Collection Study* (January 2014), http://www.dot.ri.gov (last visited May 28, 2014).

84   Shawn Foster, *Stats Show Latinos, Blacks More Likely to be Ticketed,* Salt Lake Trib., May 10, 1998, at A6.

85   *Feliciano v. County of Suffolk County,* 419 F. Supp. 2d 302 (E.D.N.Y. 2005).

86   *New York Civil Liberties Union, Report: Nypd Stop and Frisk Activity in 2011* (2012), *available at* http://www.nyclu.org/publications/report-nypd-stop-and-frisk-activity-2011-2012.

87   739 F. Supp. 2d 376 (S.D.N.Y. 2010).

DOI: 10.1057/9781137408433.0005

88 *Floyd v. City of New York*, 959 F. Supp. 2d 540, 562 (2013).

89 *Ligon v. City of New York* (In re Reassignment of Cases), 736 F.3d 118, 129 (2d Cir. 2013).

90 *Murphy v. City of Reynoldsburg*, 604 NE 2d. 138 (Ohio 1992).

91 For a discussion of the Rossano case and similar stops, see David Rudovsky, *Law Enforcement by Stereotypes and Serendipity: Racial Profiling and Stops and Searches without Cause*, Vol. 3(1) J. CONST. LAW, 296–366 (2001).

92 577 U.S. 806 (1996).

93 *Whren*, 517 U.S. at 812.

94 986 S.W. 2d 423 (Ark. Ct. App. 1999).

95 *Id.* at 428.

96 *Racial Profiling Act of 2013*, available at https:www.govtrack.us/congress/bills/113/s1038#summary.

97 CIV.A. ELH-11-3499,2013 WL 5467724 (September 30, 2013), *aff'd, Leftridge v. Doe*, 2014 U.S. App. LEXIS 6426 (4th Cir. Md., April 8, 2014).

98 *Leftridge* at 75.

99 60 U.S. (19 How.) 393 (1857).

100 Heather Schoenfeld, *The War on Drugs, the Politics of Crime, and Mass Incarceration in the United States*, 15 J. *Gender Race & Just.* 315 (2012); Jamie Fuller, *Symposium: Drug Laws; Policy and Reform; Race, Drugs, and law Enforcement in the United States*, 20 Stan. L. *Pol'y Rev* 257 (2009); John McWhorter, *How the War in Drugs Is Destroying Black America*, Cato's Letter, Winter 2011, Vol. 9 no. 1, *CATO Institute*, available at http://www.cato.org/pubs/catoletter/catoletterv9n1.pdf; Sam v. Meddis, *Is the Drug War Racist?*, *USA Today*, July 23, 1993, at A1; Ed Wiley III & Sean Jensen, *Black and Latino Males Suffer the Most in the War on Drugs, Scholar Says*, Black Issues in Higher Educ., August 12, 1993, at 9.

101 Maia Szalavitz, *Study: Whites More Likely To Abuse Drugs Than Blacks*, Time (November 7, 2011), http//healthland.time.com/2011; *U.S. Dep't of Health & Human Serv.*, National Institutes of Health, *Drug Use Among Racial/Ethnic Minorities*, Revised (2003), available at http://archives.drugabuse.gov/pubs/minorities; *National Inst. on Drug Abuse, National Household Survey on Drug Abuse: Population Estimates 1991*, at 21 (1992); *See also U.S. Depot of Health & Human Serv., Advance Rep. No. 6, Preliminary Estimate from the Drug Abuse Warning Network: January-June 1993 Preliminary Estimates of Drug-Related Emergency Room Episodes* 37 (1994) (reporting that whites have a higher number of drug abuse episodes than blacks).

102 837 F. Supp. 1386 (1993).

103 In 2010, 26.1% individuals arrested by the DEA were African-American, *see*, Mark Motivans, *U.S. Dep't of Justice, Bureau of Justice Stat., Federal Justice Statistics 2010-Statistical Tables* 6 (December 2013).

104 No. 91-5942, 1993 U.S. App. LEXIS 926 (6th Cir. 1993).

DOI: 10.1057/9781137408433.0005

105   595 F.2d 1036 (5th Cir. 1979).

106   *Id.*at 1039.

107   490 U.S. 1.

108   490 U.S. at 8–9.

109   819 F. Supp. 668 (M.D. Tenn. 1993).

110   *Jones,* 819 F. Supp. at 723.

111   837 F. Supp. 1386 (1993).

112   955 F.2d 391 (8th Cir. 1992).

113   517 U.S. 456 (1996).

114   *Armstrong,* 517 U.S. at 458.

115   *Armstrong,* 517 U.S. at 465.

116   *But see id.* 480 (Stevens, J., dissenting). Justice Stevens notes in dissent that evidence showing that "black defendants charged with distribution of crack in the Central District of California are prosecuted in federal court, whereas members of other races charged with similar offenses are prosecuted in state court." *Id.* There are differences between the federal scheme as opposed to state schemes, including the "absence of mandatory minimums, the existence of parole.... lower baseline penalties, [and that] terms of imprisonment for drug offenses tend to be substantially lower in state systems than in the federal system." *Id.* at 479. If a prosecutor chooses to prosecute a defendant in state court as opposed to federal court, this could be viewed as more favorable treatment of that defendant. *See id.* 478–480.

117   *Id.* at 466.

118   310 F.3d 1007 (7th Cir. 2002).

119   *See* Mass Incarceration, *supra* Section A; *see also People v. Coles,* 339 N.W.2d 440, 451 (1983) ("Such disparity in sentences... arises from impermissible considerations such as the race of the defendant, his economic status or personal bias and attitude of the individual sentencing judge.").

120   *See,* Tushar Kansal and Marc Mauer, *The Sentencing Project, Racial Disparity in Sentencing: A Review Literature* (January 2005), *available at* http://www. sentencingproject.org/doc/publications/rd_sentencing_review.pdf (A review of studies on racial disparities in sentencing); Samuel R. Sommers and Phoebe C. Ellsworth, *Race in the Courtroom: Perceptions of Guilt and Dispositional Attributions,* 26 PSPB 1367–1379 (November 2000) *available at* http://ase.tufts.edu/psychology/documents/pubsSommersRaceCourtroom. pdf.

121   Barbara S. Mierhoefer, *Federal Judicial Ctr., the General Effect of Mandatory Minimum Prison Terms 20* (1992), *available* at http://www.fjc.gov/public/pdf. nsf/lookup/geneffmm.pdf/$file/geneffmm.pdf.; Barbara S. Vincent and Paul J. Hofer, *Federal Judicial Center, the Consequences of Mandatory Minimum Prison Terms: A Summary of Recent Findings* (1994), *available at* http://www. fjc.gov/public/pdf.nsf/lookup/conmanmin.pdf/$file/conmanmin.pdf.

DOI: 10.1057/9781137408433.0005

122 Mark Motivans, *Office of Justice, Bureau of Statistics, Federal Justice Statistics 2010-Statistical Tables* (December 2013), *available at* http://www.bjs.gov/index.cfm?ty=pbdetail&iid=4862.

123 *American Civil Liberties Union, the War on Marijuana in Black and White,* at 4 (2013), *available at* https://www.aclu.org/criminal-law-reform/war-marijuana-black-and-white-report

124 18 U.S.C. § 3551–3673 (1988).

125 28 U.S.C. § 991 (1988).

126 28 U.S.C. § 994 (1988).

127 *U.S. General Accounting Office, Sentencing Guidelines: Central Questions Remain Unanswered 11* (1992), *available* at http://www.gao.gov/products/GGD-92-93 (hereinafter *Central Questions*).

128 *Id.* at 12–13; *see also* Gerald W. Heaney, *The Reality of Guidelines Sentencing: No End to Disparity,* 28 Am. Crim. L. Rev. 161 (1991).

129 See *Central Questions, supra* note 9, at 14–16.

130 Douglas C. Mcdonald & Kenneth E. Carlson, *Bureau of Justice Statistics, U.S. Dep't of Justice, Sentencing in the Federal Courts: Does Race Matter? the Transition to Sentencing Guidelines,* 1986–1990, at 1 (1993), *available* at https://www.ncjrs.gov/.

131 *United States Sentencing Commission, Overview of Federal Criminal Cases* (2012), *available at* http://www.ussc.gov/Research_and_Statistics/Annual_Reports_and_Sourcebooks/index.cfm.

132 David Peterson, *State Agency Reports Increase in Number of Black Drug Arrests,* Star Trib. (Minneapolis), July 9, 1992, at A1.

133 Minn. *Sentencing Guidelines Comm'n, Sentencing Practices Highlights and Statistical Tables: Felony Offenders Sentenced in 1991,* at 4 (1993); *See also* Minn. *Sentencing Guidelines Comm'n, Updated Report on Drug Offender Sentencing Issues* 1, 8–10 (2007), *available at* http://sentencing.nj.gov/downloads/pdf/articles/2007/May2007/document02.pdf. Also *see,* John Stuart and Robert Sykora, *Minnesota's Failed Experience With Sentencing Guidelines and the Future of Evidence-based Sentencing,* 37 Wm. Mitchell L. Rev. 427 (2011); *see also* Dennis Cauchon, *Sentences for Crack Called Racist, USA Today,* May 26, 1993, at 2A (finding that young black males receive longer sentences for *crack* cocaine).

134 *See* Minn. *Sentencing Guidelines Comm'n, 2014 Minn. Sentencing Guidelines Comm'n Report to the Legislature* (January 15, 2014), *available at* http://mn.gov/sentencing-guidelines.

135 *U.S. Sentencing Comm'n, Report to the Congress's Mandatory Minimum Penalties in the Federal Criminal Justice System, Brief Review of the Case Law Relating to Mandatory Minimum Sentencing Provisions, Appendix E* (October 2011), *available at* http://www.ussc.gov/sites/default/files/pdf/news/congressional-testimony-and-reports/mandatory-minimum-penalties/20111031-rtc-pdf/

Appendix_E.pdf (Outline cases challenging provision of the Act); Carissa Byrne Hessick and F. Andrew Hessick, *Recognizing Constitutional Rights at Sentencing*, 99 CALIF L. Rev. 47 (2011); Marcia G. Shein, *Racial Disparity in "Crack" Cocaine Sentencing*, 8 Crim. Just. 28, 30–31 (1993).

136   Tina L. Dorsey, ed., *U.S. Department of Justice, Bureau of Statistics, Drugs and Crime Facts* (2008), *available at* http://www.bjs.gov/content/pub/pdf/dcf. pdf; *Crack vs. Power Cocaine a Gulf in Penalties*, U.S. News, October 1, 2007, *available at* http://www.usnews.com/news/national/articles/2007/10/01/ crack-vs-powder-cocaine-a-gulf-in-penalties.

137   No. 8:Cr91-00038(02), 1993 WL 315987 (D. Neb. July 29, 1993), *convictions aff'd sub nom.*, sentences *vacated and remanded, United States v. Maxwell*, 25 F.3d 1389 (8th Cir. 1994), *cert. denied*, 115 S. Ct. 610 (1994).

138   *United States v. Maxwell*, 25 F.3d 1389 (8th Cir. 1994), *cert. denied*, 115 S. Ct. 610 (1994) (indicating that plaintiff must show the Sentencing Guidelines had a discriminatory purpose).

139   *United States v. Lattimore*, 974 F.2d 971 (8th Cir. 1992), *cert. denied*, 113 S. Ct. 1819 (1993); *United States v. Jones*, 979 F.2d 317 (3d Cir. 1992); *United States v. Galloway* 951 F.2d 64 (5th Cir. 1992); *United States v. Williams*, 962 F.2d 1218 (6th Cir. 1992). For an analysis of these earlier cases and others, see Shein, supra note 17, at 30–31. But *see, United States v. Clary*, No. 89-167-CR(4), 1994 U.S. Dist. LEXIS 2447 (E.D. Mo. February 11, 1994). In *Minnesota v. Russell*, 477 N.W.2d 886 (Minn. 1991) court declared its crack cocaine statute unconstitutional.

140   *United States Sentencing Comm'n, Report to Congress: Cocaine and Federal Sentencing Policy* (May 2002), *available at* www.ussc.gov/.../ congressional...reports/...200205...cocaine-sentencing; Michael Coyle, *The Sentencing Project, Race and Class Penalties in Crack Cocaine Sentencing* (2002), *available at* www.sentencingproject.org/.

141   For example, in 2002, African-Americans received approximately 25% of sentences issued by U.S. District Courts under the U.S. Sentencing Comm'n Guidelines. *See, Sourcebook of Criminal Justice Statistics* 432 (2003), *available at* https://www.hsdl.org/?view&did=711164; Tushar Kansal and Marc Mauer, *Racial Disparity In Sentencing: A Review of the Literature, supra* note 2; Celesta Albonetti, *Sentencing Under The Federal Sentencing Guidelines: Effect of Defendant Characteristics, Guilty Pleas, and Departures on Sentence Outcome For Drug Offense*, 31 Law & Soc'y, Rev., 789–822 (1997); Marvin Free, *The Impact of Federal Sentencing Reforms on African Americans*, 28 J. of Black Stud., 268–286 (1997).

142   Paula M. Ditton and Doris James Wilson, *Truth-in-Sentencing in State Prison, Bureau of Justice Statistics, Special Report* 1, *available at* www.bjs.gov/content/ pub/pdf/tssp.pdf.

143   *See,* Paul Finkelman, *The Crime of Color*, 67 Tul. L. Rev. 2063, 2089 (1993).

DOI: 10.1057/9781137408433.0005

144 543 U.S. 220 (2005). *Also see, Gall v. United States*, 552 U.S. 38 (2007). For a detailed analysis of the impact *Booker, see*, Crysal S. Yang, *Free at Last? Judicial Discretion and Racial Disparities in Federal Sentencing, U. Chi. L.Sch., Chi. Unbound* (October 2013), *available at* chicagounbound.uchicago. edu/.../viewcontent.cgi?.

145 132 S. Ct. 2321 (2012).

146 *Id.* at 2328.

147 Testimony of Attorney General Eric H. Holder, Jr. Urges Changes in Federal Sentencing Guidelines to Reserve Harshest Penalties for Most Serious Drug Traffickers (May 13, 2014), *available at* http:www.justice. gov/printf/printout3.jsp.

148 719 F. 3d 482, 485 (2013).

149 *Id.* at 486.

150 *U.S. Dep't of Justice, Office of Public Affairs, Attorney General Holder: Justice Department Set to Expand Clemency Criteria Will Prepare for Wave of Applications from Drug Offenders in Federal Prison* (April 21, 2014), *available at* http://www.justice.gov/.

151 *U.S. Sentencing Comm'n, the Federal Sentencing Guidelines: A Report on the Operation of the Guidelines System and Short-Term Impacts on Disparity in Sentencing, Use of Incarceration, and Prosecutorial Discretion and Plea Bargaining* 65 (1991), www.ussc.gov/ (last visited May 28, 2014).

152 Charles P. Bubany & Frank Skillern, *Taming the Dragon: An Administrative Law for Prosecutorial Decision-Making*, 13 Am. crim. L. Rev. 473, 476–489 (1976).

153 Angela J. Davis, *In Search of Racial Justice: The Role of the Prosecutor*, 16 N.Y.U. J. Legis. & Pub. Pol'y 821 (2013); Angela J. Davis, *Prosecution and Race! The Power and Privilege of Discretion*, 67 Fordham L. Rev. 13 (1998); Ruth Marcus, *Racial Bias Widely Seen in Criminal Justice System, Research Often Supports Black Perception, WashIngton Post*, May 12, 1992, at A4 (citing a study conducted in San Jose which indicated that blacks found it more difficult to plea bargain than whites).

154 Besiki Kutateladze et al.; *Vera Inst. of Justice, Do Race and Ethnicity Matter in Prosecution? A Review of Empirical Studies*, 13–14 (2012), *available at* http;// www. Vera.org/sites/default/files/resources/downloads/race-and-ethnicity/-in-prosecutor first-edition.pdf. *Also see*, generally *Developments in the Law: Race and the Criminal Process*, 101 Harv. L. Rev. 1472, 1525–1529 (1988) (discussing multiple studies).

155 See Martha A. Myers & John A. Hogan, *Prosecutors and the Allocation of Court Resources*, 26 Soc. Probs. 439, 446 (1979).

156 See Bob Levenson & Debbie Salamone, *Prosecutors See Death Penalty in Black and White, Orlando Sentinel Trib.*, May 24, 1992, at A1; Robert Bohn, *Race and the Death Penalty in the United States*, in *Race and Criminal Justice* 71, 81

DOI: 10.1057/9781137408433.0005

(Michael J. Lynch & E. Britt Patterson eds, 1991) (citing a number of studies on state prosecutors which find racial bias in prosecutorial decisions to charge a defendant with a capital crime).

157   Michael L. Radelet & Glenn L. Pierce, *Race and Prosecutorial Discretion in Homicide Cases*, 19 L. & Soc. Rev. 587, 615–619 (1985). In *McCleskey v. Kemp*, 481 U.S. 279 (1987), a study of the death penalty determined that prosecutors sought the death penalty in 70% of the cases involving black defendants and white victims; 15% of the cases involving black defendants and black victims; and 19% of the cases involving white defendants and black victims. The court nevertheless ruled against McCleskey.

158   *McCleskey v. Kemp*, 481 U.S. 279, 313, 1987.

159   Angela J. Davis, *In Search of Racial Justice: The Role of the Prosecutor*, 16 N.Y.U. J. Legis. & Pub. Pol'y 821 (2013).

160   See, http://www.vera.org/centers/prosecution-and racial justice-program.

161   Besiki Kutateladze et al.; *Vera Inst. of Justice, Do Race and Ethnicity Matter in Prosecution, supra* note 3.

162   Cassia Spohn et al., *The Impact of the Ethnicity and Gender of Defendants on the Decision to Reject or Dismiss Felony Charges*, 25 *Criminology* 175 (1987).

163   Sonjs B. Star and M. Marit Rehavi, *Mandatory Sentencing and Racial Disparity: Assessing the Role of Prosecutors and the Effects of Brooker*, 123 Yale L. J.1 (2013), *available at* http://www.yalelawjournal.org/article/mandatory-sentencing-and-racial-disparity-assessing-the-role-of-prosecutors-and-the-effects-of-booker; Sonja B. Star and M. Marit Rehavi, *Racial Disparity in Federal Criminal Charging and Its Sentencing Consequences, University of Michigan Law School*, 2012, *available at* http://www.fjc.gov/public/pdf.nsf/lookup/NSPI201213.pdf/$file/NSPI201213.

164   See *Aba Comm. on Racial & Ethnic Diversity in the Prof., Statistics about Minorities in the Profession from the Census, available at* http://www.abanet. org/minorities/ links/2000census.html (last visited May 26, 2024) Ellen J. Pollock & Stephen J. Adler, *Legal System Struggles to Reflect Diversity, But Progress Is Slow, Wall St. J.*, May 8, 1992, at A1 (finding that defendant's lawyer, the prosecutor, and the judge will not be black). "Michigan's prosecutor's offices are overwhelmingly populated by white males."

165   Pollock & Adler, *supra* note 14, at A1.

166   See Laurie L. Levinson, *The Future of State and Federal Civil Rights Prosecutors: The Lessons of the Rodney King Trial*, 41 UCLA L. Rev. 509, 562 (1994).

167   *See Report of the Indep. Comm'n on the L.a. Police Dep't* 3-7 [hereinafter CHRISTOPHER REPORT] (1991), *available at* www.parc.info/ . . . /Special%20 Reports/1%20-%20Chistopher%20Commision. Pdf.

168   Terry McMillan, *This is America, N.Y. Times*, May 1, 1992, at A35.

169   *See* Lee A. Daniels, *Some of the Jurors Speak, Giving Sharply Differing Views, N.Y. Times*, May 1, 1992, at A10 (stating that one juror believed that King

DOI: 10.1057/9781137408433.0005

was in control of the situation. "[A]s long as he fought the patrolman, the policeman had to continue to try to maintain him, to keep from having more erratic felonious action."").

170 *Detroit Police Beat Motorist to Death: 7 Officers Suspended in Case That Harks Back to Rodney King,* THE HOUSTON CHRON., November 7, 1992, at A1.

171 Id.; see also *Detroit Settles with Beating Victim's Family,* CHI. TRIB., June 10, 1994, at 27 (discussing that the Detroit City Council approved a $5.25 million settlement for a civil action filed by Green's family).

172 *Police Force: Hall of Famer Awarded $540,000 in a Suit Against L.A.P.D.,* A.B.A.J. May 1991, at 25; Crack Down Hard on Police Brutality, USA TODAY, March 21, 1991, at 12A; see also *Christopher Report, supra* note 1, at 56 ("From 1986 through 1990 the City paid in excess of $20 million... in over 300 lawsuits... alleging excessive use of force [by police]").

173 Paul W. Valentine, *$1.9 Million Awarded in Beating: Pr. George's Officers Found Culpable in Fatal 1989 Arrest, Washington Post,* March 17, 1993, at A1.

174 George Lardner, Jr., *McDuffie Death: It Seemed to be Open-Shut Case, Washington Post,* May 21, 1980, at A1.

175 Barbara Carmen, City Settles Lawsuit: OSU Student Will Receive $170,000 for Force in Arrest, COLUMBUS DISPATCH, June 9, 1992, at 1A; Bruce Cadwallader & Catherine Candishky, L.A. Beating Puts Local Policeman Case in Spotlight, *Columbus Dispatch,* March 22, 1991, at 7B.

176 Tamer-El-Ghobashy, *$ 7 Million Payout in Sean Bell Case, Wall St. J.,* July 28, 2010, *available at* htt://online.wsj.com/news/articles

177 Jason Grotto, Hal Dardick, and Heather Gillers, *Mayor Seeks to Borrow Up to $900 Million More,* April 19, 2014 at 57, *available at* http://articles. chicagotribune.com/2014-02-03/news/ct-met-bonds-new-chicago-borrowing-20140204_1_tax-increases-city-leaders-finance-committee (part of which will be used to pay off police brutality cases).

178 Tracy L. Snell, *U.S. Department of Justice. Bureau of Justice Statistics, Capital Punishment, 2011-Statistical Tables 1* (July 2013), *available at* http://www.bjs. gov/index.cfm?ty=pbdetail&iid=4697.

179 *Id.*

180 *Naacp Legal Def. & Educ. Fund, Criminal Justice Project, Death Row Usa 62* (Winter 2013), *available at* http://www.naacpldf.org/files/publications/ DRUSA_Winter_2013.pdf.

181 *See, Ohioans to Stop Executions, the Death Lottery; How Race and Geography Determine Who Goes to Ohio's Death Row* (April 1, 2014), *available at* www. otse.org/wp-content/.../04/OTSE-Report-The-Death-Lottery.pdf.

182 *Death Penalty: Hearings Before the Senate Judiciary Comm. on S. 32,* 101st Cong., 1st Sess. 938 (1991). (More than 20 years later, the disparities still exit in how death penalty policies are implemented.)

183 *Furman v. Georgia,* 408 U.S. 238, 249–250 (1972).

DOI: 10.1057/9781137408433.0005

184   *United States v. Wiley*, 492 F.2d 547, 555 (5th Cir. 1973) (Bazelon, C. J., concurring).

185   481 U.S. 279 (1987).

186   David C. Baldus et al., *Equal Justice and the Death Penalty* 406–407 (1990).

187   *Georgia and the Nation, Race and The Death Penalty* (ACLU/Capital Punishment, New York, N.Y.), Fall 1987, at 1–2; *McCleskey*, 481 U.S. at 321–322.

188   *McCleskey*, 481 U.S. at 292.

189   114 S. Ct. 1127 (1994).

190   *Id.* at 319.

191   *See* Hans Zeisel, Race *Bias in the Administrations of the Death Penalty: The Florida Experience*, 95 Harv. L. Rev. 456, 458–461, 468 (1988).

192   21 U.S.C. § 848(o)(2) (1988).

193   *U.S. Gen. Accounting Office, Death Penalty Sentencing: Research Indicates Pattern of Racial Disparities* 5–6 (1990).

194   *Sen. Hearings on Death Penalty, supra* note 132; *Death Sentencing Issues, Hearings Before the Subcomm. on Civil and Constitutional Rights*, 102d Cong., 1st Sess. (1991) [hereinafter *House Hearings on Death Sentencing*].

195   *House Hearings on Death Sentencing, supra* note 17, at 211, 214–216, 220–227.

196   Senate Bill 461. For a detailed discussion of the Act *see*, Barbara O'Brien and Catherine M. Grosso, *Confronting Race: How a Confluence of Social Movements Convinced North Carolina to go Where the McCleskey Court Wouldn't*, 2011 Mich. St. L. Rev. 463 (2011). Also *see* Kentucky Racial Justice Act of 1998, Ky. Rev. Stat. Ann. § 532.300 (West 2013); In Ohio a task force on the death penalty has recommended the enactment of Racial Justice Act, *see Joint Task Force to Review the Administration of Ohio's Death Penalty, Final Report & Recommendations* (April 2014), *available at* www.sc.ohio.gov/Boards/deathPenalty/resources/finalReport.pdf.

197   *Id.*

198   *State v. Robinson*, No. CRS 23143 (N.C. Super. Ct. Apr. 20, 2012). For a detailed discussion of the Robinson case, *see* John Powers, *State v. Robinson and the Racial Justice Act: Statistical Evidence of Racial Discrimination in Capital Proceedings*, 29 Harv. J. Racial & Ethnic Just. 117 (Spring, 2013).

199   Barbara O'brien and Catherine M. Grosso, *Report on Jury Selection Study, Michigan University College of Law*, September 29, 2011, *available at* www.aclu.org/…/jss_revised_report_with_appendix_29_sept_2011.pdf-.

200   *State v. Robinson, supra* note 21.

201   *See*, Michael L. Radelet and Glenn L. Pierce, *Race and Death Sentencing in North Carolina, 1980–2000*, N. C. L. Rev., 89 2120 (2011).

202   *House Hearings on Death Sentencing*, at 17 (statement of Gary Parker, Esq., Columbus, Ga.).

DOI: 10.1057/9781137408433.0005

203 *A National Agenda for Children: On the Front Lines with Attorney General Janet Reno, Juvenile Justice* (U.S. Dep't of Justice/Office of Juvenile Justice and Delinquency Prevention, Washington, D.C.), Fall/Winter 1993, at 30 (stating that "[b]lack youth were six times more likely to be victims of homicide than white youth").

204 *U.S. Department of Justice, Office of Juvenile Justice and Delinquency Prevention, Juvenile Arrest 2011* (December 2013), *available at* http://www.ojjdp.gov/publications/PubResults.asp?sei=86; Jerome G. Miller, *Search & Destroy: The Plight of African-American Males in the Criminal Justice System* 19 (1993).

205 *Juvenile Arrest 2011, supra* note 204. *Also see, The Sentencing Project, Disproportionate Minority Contact in the Juvenile Justice System* (May 2014), *available at* www.sentencingproject.org/ ... Disproportionate%20 Minority%20Contact.pdf.

206 *See* Christopher S. Dunn et al., *Bowling Green State University, Race and Juvenile Justice in Ohio: The Overrepresentation and Disproportionate Confinement of African American and Hispanic Youth* 3–8 (June 1993) (unpublished report, on file with author) (finding that minority youth in Ohio, especially African-American males, are overrepresented and disproportionately confined).

207 Ted Tollett & Billy R. Close, *The Overrepresentation of Blacks in Florida's Juvenile Justice System,* in *Race & Criminal Justice* 86, 87–88 (Michael J. Lynch & E. Britt Patterson eds, 1991). *Report and Recommendations of the Florida Supreme Court Racial and Ethnic Bias Study Commission* (1990), *reprinted in* 19 *Fla. St. U. L. Rev.* 591, 601 (1992).

208 *Office of Program Accountability, Bureau of Research and Planning, Florida Department of Juvenile Justice, Delinquency in Florida's Schools; a Seven-Year Study (Fy 2004–2005 through Fy 2010–2011)* (November 2011), *available at* http://www.djj.state.fl.us/docs/research2/2010-11-delinquency-in-schools-analysis.pdf?sfvrsn=0.

209 Charlyn Bohland, *Comments: No longer a Child: Juvenile Incarceration in America,* 39 *Cap. U. L. Rev.* 193 (Winter 2011); *U.S. Department of Health and Human Services, What Challenges Are Boys Facing, and What Opportunities Exist to Address Those Challenges*; Fact Sheet, Juvenile Delinquency, 2000, *available* at http://aspe.hhs.gov/hsp/08/boys/factsheets/jd/report.pdf.

210 *See* Charles Puzzanchera and Sean Addie, *U.S. Department of Justice, Ojjdp, Delinquency Cases Waived to Criminal Court, 2010* (February 2014), *available at* http://www.ncjj.org/Publication/Delinquency-Cases-Waived-to-Criminal-Court-2010.aspx; OJJDP, *National Series: Juveniles in Corrections, available at* https://www.ncjrs.gov/html; Jeffrey Fagan et al., *Racial Determinants of the Judicial Transfer Decision: Prosecuting Violent Youth in Criminal Court,* 33 *Crime & Delinq.* 259, 259 (1987) (citing a number of studies which find that minority youth, particularly males, are transferred to adult court); M.A.

DOI: 10.1057/9781137408433.0005

Bortner, *Traditional Rhetoric, Organizational Realities: Remand of Juveniles to Adult Court*, 32 *Crime & Delinq.* 53, 71 n.5 (1986); Robert B. Keiter, *Criminal or Delinquent?: A Study of Juvenile Cases Transferred to the Criminal Court*, 19 *Crime & Delinq.* 528, 532 (1973) (finding that the profile of a juvenile transferred from Cook County Juvenile to the Criminal Court "was likely to be a black male near the age of sixteen").

211 *Juvenile Justice Initiative, Automatic Adult Prosecution of Children in Cook County, Illinois*, 2010–2012 (April 2014), *available* at http://www.modelsforchange.net/publications/532.

212 Antoinette Davis, Angela Irvine, & Jason Ziedenberg, *Stemming the Flow of Youth into Adult Systems* (March 31, 2014), *available at* http://nccdglobal.org/sites/default/files/publication_pdf/adult-transfer-info-sheet.pdf.

213 *Action for Children; from Push Out to Lock Up: North Carolina's Accelerated School-to-Prisoner Pipeline (2013)*, *available at* http://www.ncchild.org/content/push-out-lock-north-carolinas-accelerated-school-prison-pipeline; Also see, *Justice Center, the Council of State Government, Breaking Schools' Rules: A Statewide Study of How School Discipline Relates to Students' Success and Juvenile Justice Involvement (2011)*, *available at* http://knowledgecenter.csg.org/kc/content/breaking-schools-rules-statewide-study.

214 *U.S. Department of Justice, Office of Public Affairs, Justice Department Files Lawsuit in Mississippi to Protect the Constitutional Rights of Children* (October 24, 2012), *available at* http:??www.justice.gov/printf/PrintOut3.jso.

3

Civil Justice System and Other Institutional Systems

Abstract: *This chapter presents evidence that African-American males are disproportionately harmed not only by every aspect of the criminal justice system but also by other institutional systems. Specifically, from education, employment, voting, and health care services, African-American males face racial injustices. The status of African-American males in public schools continues to deteriorate at an alarming rate. It is clear that at every step of the educational system, from preschool to college African-American males face almost insurmountable challenges to complete high school and to attend college. The rate of unemployment and underemployment for African-American males has worsened during the past four decades, in part because of discrimination. They also face voting disenfranchisement. Indeed, every year, approximately 1.4 million African-American males' ability to vote in this country has been abridged temporarily or permanently. This chapter also confirms that African-American males face racial disparity in receiving health services.*

Weatherspoon, Floyd. *African-American Males and the U.S. Justice System of Marginalization: A National Tragedy.* New York: Palgrave Macmillan, 2014.
DOI: 10.1057/9781137408433.0006.

3.1   The status of African-American males in public schools

The status of African-American males in public schools continues to deteriorate at an alarming rate. At every step of the educational system, from preschool to college, African-American males face almost insurmountable challenges.

Fifty years after the decision in *Brown v. Board of Education*,[1] the status of African-American males in public schools has only improved marginally; indeed in some cases it has deteriorated. African-American male students are stereotyped as deviant, hostile, and oppositional. The Supreme Court decisions in *Brown vs. Board of Education* only changed the physical location of where African-American males were educated, from segregated to desegregated systems. In this transition, African-American males continue to lag behind in every educational performance level. Now that schools have returned to primarily segregated systems, the achievement gaps between African-American male students and white male students continue to widen.

A 2014 report by CNN revealed that some college players could only read at the fourth grade level.[2] Far too many African-American athletics are passed along, even though they have educational deficiencies. It appears that these types of educational experiences are not an anomaly but a pattern of educational deficiencies of African-American male students through the country. A wealth of statistical data on the status of African-American males in public schools supports this conclusion. As early as elementary school, African-American male students are disproportionately labeled as hyperactive, and labeled as special needs students. By the fourth grade, African-American males are on dysfunctional tracks to fail in public schools. In elementary schools, African-American male students are systematically isolated and segregated within the school. The isolation and marginalization of African-American males may be a motivating factor for the large numbers of African-American males who drop out of school and even commit suicide.

Educational studies have suggested that African-American male students have different learning styles, motivators, and cultural differences which may conflict with the traditional method of teaching and educational models. Clearly, there is a major need in reforming our educational system to meet the needs of all students, specifically the various subgroups, which include African-American males.

DOI: 10.1057/9781137408433.0006

In addition, economic disparity may further frustrate and isolate black male students who are placed in not only predominately white middle-class environments, but also predominately black educational environments which rely totally on a European model of teaching. It is not to suggest that African-American males have not made significant accomplishments in education since *Brown*, but just the opposite. What is clear is that their accomplishments lag substantially behind the educational accomplishments of other groups. African-American males are normally listed among the most negative educational statistical data collected and reported. The most troubling educational statistics on African-American males relate to graduation rates, dropout rates, suspension and expulsion rates, placement in special education classes, low test scores, and lack of placement in advance placement classes. Indeed, African-American males' academic progression in public schools has leveled off, if not remained stagnant. The following educational data on their rate of graduation, dropout, suspension and expulsion rates, placement in special education classes, and exclusion in advance courses illustrate their underclass status in public schools.

3.1.1   Graduation rates

The overall graduation rate of African-American students is deplorable. The Schott Foundation reports that the 2009–2010 national graduation rate for white male students was 78%, whereas African-American male students' graduation rate was 52%.[3] The reports also indicate that in some school districts, the graduation rate for African-American males is substantially less than the national rate. For example, Detroit has one of the lowest graduation rates for African-American males of 20%. In Cleveland the graduation rate is 28% and in Philadelphia it is 24%.

When one reviews the graduation rates of African-American males reported by each state, the disparity is startling. In virtually every state, regardless of which part of the country, African-American males' graduation rate is disproportionately lower than that of whites. Interestingly, the graduation rate of African-American males is lower in some school districts in the Northeast than in the South. With the long history of racial segregation in the South, the thought would be that their graduation rate would be lower than in any other region of the country.

Statistical educational data support that the graduation rate for African-American males is in crisis. African-American male students

DOI: 10.1057/9781137408433.0006

are missing in the statistical data which represents success and academic achievements. African-American males are in lower grades than white students based on their age. In addition, African-American males are more likely to repeat grades than white males. Moreover, African-American males rarely graduate valedictorians of their high school class, nor are they recognized for scholastic achievements.

Starting in elementary school, the failure of public schools to educate African-American males negatively impacts their economic and social status in society. Their negative educational experience in turn affects their employment abilities. Surprisingly, many school districts do not collect statistical data on various subgroups, for example, African-American males, thus making it difficult to track and verify racial and gender disparities in the school system. Consequently, the graduation rates and progress of African-American males in public schools may be worse than what is presently reported.

3.1.2 Dropout rates

The dropout rate has marginally decreased for African-American males during the past 20 years; however, the dropout rates of African-American males still remain high in comparison with those of white students. The dropout rate of African-American male students in high school is disproportionately higher than other groups of students. The National Center of Education Statistics reported that in 2012, white males' dropout rate was 4.8%, whereas that of African-American males was 8.1%.[4] In some school districts, the dropout rate for African-American males is higher than 50% and has become an endemic problem facing African-American male students. According to the U.S. Census Bureau, in 2009 the dropout rate for African-Americans aged 18–24 years was 11.6%, whereas the dropout rate for whites the same age was 9.7%.[5] Practically every state reports that African-American students, particularly African-American males, disproportionately drop out of school. One study suggested that the dropout rate for African-American males is even worse than what is reported if the numbers included the high number of males incarcerated who failed to complete high school.[6]

There is no one reason why African-American males drop out of high school. Clearly, among the reasons has to be a curriculum that fails to motivate and stimulate African-American males in a way that they appreciate the immediate benefits of an education.

DOI: 10.1057/9781137408433.0006

The strict enforcement of school policies on zero tolerance for various infractions has had a direct correlation to African-American male students being expelled and/or suspended, which may encourage them to drop out of school permanently. Even more disheartening is that some studies have suggested that the student dropout rates have a correlation to incarceration rates.

The absence of African-American male teachers to inspire, motivate, and encourage African-American male students to remain in school may also have a negative impact on their desire to stay in school and graduate. Too often, the one or two African-American male teachers also serve as coaches and are primarily focused on the upcoming sport season, not the academic success of African-American males. With no support from home, school, or community, African-American male students may drop out and seek their acceptance among other African-American male dropouts. The long-term effect will be lower wages, longer periods of unemployment, underemployment, and positions without benefits or pensions.

3.1.3   Disproportionate suspensions and expulsions

Numerous educational studies and school district records support the conclusion that African-American male students in public schools throughout the country are disproportionately suspended and expelled from school. It has reached an epidemic status.[7] For example, in 2011, the U.S. Department of Education's Office of Civil Rights reported that a number of school districts around the country have also compiled studies which conclude that African-American students, particularly males, are disproportionately suspended and expelled. The Department of Education has also determined that "[b]lack students are suspended and expelled at a rate three times greater than white students. On average, 5% of white students are suspended, compared to 16% of black students."[8] This evidence overwhelming supports the conclusion that African-American students, particularly males, are far more likely to be suspended or expelled compared to their peers.

When school districts report suspension and expulsion by subgroups, African-American males will be among the highest group suspended and expelled. In 2010, nine middle schools in Nashville suspended half of their black male student population and six middle schools had only suspended African-American males.[9] Further, a 2010–2011 study of the

DOI: 10.1057/9781137408433.0006

Oakland Unified School District reported that African-American males were suspended at a rate of five to eight times that of white males, and approximately 20 percent of the African-American males had been suspended at least once in the previous year.[10] In Palm Beach County, Florida, reports indicate that the suspension rate for black males exceeded 50%.[11]

According to a study published by Yale University, even long before high school, African-American males are disproportionately suspended from preschool and kindergarten. This trend continues throughout the African-American males' educational experience. A study by the National Center for Education Statistics reported that:

> In 1999, 35 percent of Black students in grades 7 through 12 had been suspended or expelled at some point in their school careers, higher than the 20 percent of Hispanics and 15 percent of Whites.[12]

Approximately 15 years later, African-American students are still at more risk of being suspended in school than whites. A study by the Equity Project at Indiana University of suspension rates in middle schools at 18 urban school districts determined that:

> [f]or middle school Blacks, 28.3% of males and 18% of females were suspended. This 10-point difference in suspension rates by gender for Black students was the largest of any racial group, but all racial/ethnic groups showed large internal differences by gender. Even greater disparities existed between racial groups when comparing suspension rates by race and gender: there was a 26.2 percentage point difference between the suspension rates of Asian American/Pacific Islander females (2.1%) and Black males.[13]

A study by the Center for Civil Rights Remedies at UCLA identified a number of sites where African-American male students are at risk of being suspended at extreme rates. The study described these school districts as "hotspots." A sampling of where African-American males are at risk of being suspended includes Chicago (75%), Memphis City (59%), Los Angeles (41%), Houston (44%), and Dallas (65%).[14] These numbers reflect that African-American male students are on track in these school systems to drop out of school or if they return will be less engaging than other students without a record of suspensions. They will be invisible until they are suspended again.

Not only are African-American males disproportionately suspended, often their suspensions are more severe than those of other students. The *Brown* decision eliminated *de jure* segregation and forced schools

DOI: 10.1057/9781137408433.0006

to desegregate but *Brown* failed to protect African-American males for being disproportionately suspended in predominantly white schools. Whether the school district is located in the South, North, East, or West, African-American male students will be at the top of the statistical data for school suspensions and expulsions. The disproportionate rate of suspensions and expulsions of African-American males may violate state constitutional provisions, which often require a fundamental right to an education. Such practices may also violate Title VI of the Civil Rights Act of 1964. There is no definitive study which explains why African-American males are disproportionately suspended and expelled from school; however, in *Hawkins v. Coleman*,[15] the court determined that African-American students were disproportionately suspended because of "institutional racism."

School districts still intentionally or unintentionally rely on discriminatory factors in administrating disciplinary actions.[16] There are a number of indicators that have been identified as having a negative impact on African-American males. For example, the disproportionate number of African-American males suspended or expelled may be the result of race, plus gender, and stereotyping.

The issue of stereotyping was alleged in *Fuller v. Decatur Public School Board of Education*.[17] In *Fuller*, six high school age African-American male students were expelled for fighting at a football game. The students alleged that they were expelled because "they were stereotyped as gang members and racially profiled by the actions of the School Board." Similarly, in *Lee v. Butler County Board of Education*,[18] testimony was presented that African-American males "were being disproportionately disciplined." Nevertheless, the court granted the school board's motion to declare the school system a unitary status, thus ending the school desegregation litigation. The court accepted the superintendent's testimony that the school was primarily African-American, but failed to explore the race plus sex theory. The courts failed to determine whether African-American males were disproportionately receiving more disciplinary actions, as well as more severe disciplinary actions than any other group.

The U.S. Department of Education should require every school district to analyze suspension and expulsion data according to race plus gender. This would determine whether African-American males are disproportionately receiving disciplinary actions in schools. Moreover, school districts should determine whether their suspension and expulsion

DOI: 10.1057/9781137408433.0006

policies have a disparate impact on African-American boys, and if so, explore other options in place of suspensions.[19]

The disproportionate numbers of African-American males suspended and expelled from school also have a direct impact on the disproportionate numbers of African-American males in the juvenile court system, low graduation rates, low grades, and their motivation to remain in school. School districts have a moral and legal obligation to develop alternatives to reduce the suspension and expulsion rate of African-American males from schools. In early 2014, the Justice Department and the Department of Education issued guidance to school districts on how to implement disciplinary policies in a nondiscriminatory manner. The federal government's effort will bring attention to school district the urgency of reducing the racial disproportionality of suspension and expulsion practices in public schools.[20]

3.1.4   Exclusion in honor and college prep classes

African-American students are systematically excluded from honor classes, college prep courses, and gifted programs. They are more often placed on a special education track and excluded from educational tracks designed for advanced placement and gifted programs. For example, in *Thomas County Branch of the NAACP v. City of Thomasville School District*,[21] the court determined that the practice of "ability group" or "tracking" a disproportionate number of African-American students were placed in the "lower ability group," thus were not placed in the academically advanced classes. The court stated:

> Tragically, it appears that for many of these children, the "die is cast" as early as kindergarten. These children do not appear to be reevaluated (and thus potentially re-tracked during their progressions through the system.[22]

The court, nevertheless, held that there was no evidence that the school district intentionally used the tracking system to exclude African-American students from certain classes. In essence, the court sanctioned a system that maintains the segregation of students on the basis of race. The white students are assigned to advance courses and minorities are assigned to low-ability classes. Approximately thirty years before the decision in the *City of Thomasville School District*, the court in *Hobson v. Hansen*[23] had held that African-American students were discriminately tracked into lower level, less challenging schools. Unfortunately, many school districts still have continued this practice of segregating African-American students into general education courses.

The exclusion of African-American students from advanced courses is not always blatant, but more often subtle. This subtlety was obvious in a case brought against the Rockford Board of Education,[24] in Rockford, Illinois, where the plaintiffs, African-Americans and Hispanics, argued that while the school may be desegregated, classrooms within the school were still segregated. The plaintiffs argued that minority students were underrepresented in advanced courses. In dismissing this claim, the court reasoned that minorities had an opportunity to enroll in such cases. Specifically, the court stated:

> It is provincial and naïve to suppose that because [the school district] once engaged in de facto segregation of its public schools, the choices of its minority students regarding voluntary enrollment in advanced classes open to all are a legacy of that segregation.[25]

The court clearly indicated a lack of understanding of the long-term negative impact that segregation and isolation can have on minority students. The mere fact that a school board announces that they are no longer excluding minorities from advance classes, where in the past white students were nourished, mentored, and encouraged to take such courses, will not, without more, eradicate the present effect of past discrimination. The inference that only white students are capable of taking such courses may linger until school districts take positive actions to ensure that minorities, especially African-American males, feel welcome in such classes. Moreover, the use of tracking maintains segregation within a school system.

African-American males are systematically excluded from taking advance courses in science, mathematics, and foreign languages. These courses are considered college preparatory courses which may lead to acceptance in college, scholarships, and advanced placement. These exclusions may be intentional on the part of teachers as part of a stereotypical bias that African-American males lack the intelligence, motivation, and support from their parents to be successful. Teachers may reinforce their stereotypical biases by projecting low expectations for achievement toward African-American male students, which becomes a self-fulfilling prophecy. African-American males are more likely to be placed in lower, less challenging educational tracks. Likewise, African-

DOI: 10.1057/9781137408433.0006

American males are more likely to be taking remedial mathematics and general English.

In addition to being excluded from honor classes, they are absent from honor- and academic-related organizations. From elementary school to college, African-American males are intensely recruited to play school sports but are not recruited or encouraged to join or participate in academic school clubs and organizations. For example, African-American males are less likely than whites to be identified as "gifted" to participate in gifted educational programs. Often, these programs are not well publicized and are secretly shared with a select group of parents. Students are selected based on a teacher's recommendation. These programs permit students to participate in a variety of enrichment programs, as well as placement in advance course. Unlike in sports, African-American males are not groomed and actively recruited for these programs. School systems which intentionally exclude African-American students from gifted and college prep programs may be in violation of Title VI of the Civil Rights Act of 1964.

The systematic exclusion and isolation of African-American males from gifted school programs perpetuates the stereotypical biases that African-American males are only interested in sports. It also further perpetuates their perceived academic inferiority. In the Supreme Court decision of *Strauder v. West Virginia*,[26] Justice Strong expressed the concern that the exclusion of African-American men from serving as jurors was like permanently placing a brand of inferiority on them in violation of the law. The overplacement of African-American males in special education programs, and the practice of systematically excluding them from advance courses, forever brands them as inferior among other students and teachers.[27]

3.1.5   Overrepresentation in special education classes

Far too many African-American male boys are assigned to special education classes and graduate with special education diplomas. It was never the intentions of the Supreme Court's decision in *Brown* that African-American students, especially African-American males, would be segregated by race in schools and further segregated by race plus gender in special education classes. The segregation of African-American males into special education classes and tracking programs negatively impacts their self-esteem, progress in school, and ultimately their rates

DOI: 10.1057/9781137408433.0006

of dropout and graduation. The disproportionate placement of African-American males in special education programs further subordinates their status in public schools. Moreover, the disproportionate assignment of African-American males in special education classes further perpetuates stereotypical biases that African-American male students who have behavioral issues are automatically labeled as being mentally challenged and academically deficient.

Numerous studies and reports by leading researchers have determined that minority students are overrepresented in special education school programs.[28] Additionally, the U.S. Department of Education, Office of Civil Rights, the agency that investigates discrimination in school systems receiving federal funds, has determined that school systems disproportionately assign African-American students to special education curriculum. For example, in some states, 25% of African-American males are in special education programs. Even more disturbing is that in some school districts, African-American males represent more than 40% of students classified as special education. African-American students comprise 20% of the population of students receiving special education services.

The reasons for the disproportionate number of minorities placed in special education are many. The list includes such factors as the "misidentified and misuse of tests," the "failure of the general education system," and "insufficient resources." There is also a concern that teachers may place African-American male students in special education programs as a disciplinary action. Assigning African-American males to special education classes may also defeat their motivation for completing school. For example, the Wisconsin Department of Public Instruction reported "the highest dropout rate for students with disabilities is for black males at 15.78%."

In 1975, Congress passed the Individuals with Disabilities Act (IDEA) to ensure that students with disabilities would have "...a free appropriate public school education which emphasizes social education and related services designed to meet their unique needs." Prior to the passage of the IDEA, many school districts failed to provide disabled individuals with an adequate public education, if any at all. For example, in *Mills v. Board of Education of the District of Columbia*,[29] six of the seven minority plaintiffs were African-American male students who challenged the school board's practice of excluding them and other disabled students from adequate public schools and facilities. The court held in *Mills* that

DOI: 10.1057/9781137408433.0006

disabled children have a constitutional right to a free and appropriate education (FAPE).

Unfortunately, the IDEA has been at times a double-edged sword. In other words, it has been overly used to label and disproportionately place African-American males in special education programs and out of mainstream educational instruction. At the same time, African-American males with mental disabilities have been suspended and expelled from school in lieu of receiving services required by the IDEA. Even though it was quite obvious to educators and researchers that minorities were disproportionately placed in special education programs, the federal government did not respond in any meaningful manner until 1997, when they passed the amendments to IDEA. The Amendments state that "greater efforts are needed to prevent the intensification of problems connected with mislabeling and high dropout rates among minority children with disabilities." Notwithstanding the Amendment, minorities, particularly African-American males, are still often mislabeled and disproportionately drop out of school. The IDEA was reauthorized and amended in 2004.

Standardized intelligence tests, otherwise known as IQ tests, are used to determine the placement of students in special education classes. The use of IQ tests was challenged in *Larry P. v. Riles*.[30] In *Riles*, African-American elementary school children challenged the use of the State of California's IQ test which resulted in a disproportionate number of African-American students to be placed in special education classes. The District Court held that the State had used tests which were "racially and culturally biased, and had a discriminatory impact against black children" in violation of Title VI of the Civil Rights Act of 1964, the Rehabilitation Act of 1973, and the Education for all Handicapped Children Act of 1975. The Court expressed concern with permanently placing African-American students "into educationally dead-end, isolated, and stigmatizing classes." More than twenty years later, African-American students, especially African-American males, are still disproportionately placed in such classes.

Similarly, in *Parents in Action on Special Education v. Hannon*,[31] African-American parents challenged the use of standardized intelligence tests administered by the Chicago Board of Education as being culturally biased toward African-American students. The parents presented evidence that African-American students were disproportionately placed in the educable mentally handicapped classes. As a result of the test, 80% of the students in the educable mentally handicapped classes were African-American students. Even though the Judge recognized that there were a few questions on the intelligence tests that were "culturally biased against black children, or at least sufficiently suspect," nevertheless, the court held that these few questions would not invalidate the test. Unfortunately, a negative impact of the *Brown* decision was that African-American students, especially African-American males who were assigned to desegregated schools, were disproportionately labeled with having a mental disability and "dumped" into special education classes. Ostensibly, they were assigned to such classes to receive specialized educational assistance, but in reality they were warehoused and passed on through the system. Similarly, African-American males who attend segregated schools are warehoused and segregated in special education classes. The overrepresentation of African-American males in special education is the result of them being misidentified, labeled, and placed in an inappropriate educational track.

3.1.6   Proficiency and achievement tests

African-American males trail whites and African-American female students in every aspect of education achievement tests. Specifically, African-American girls outperform African-American boys and white boys outperform both groups. For example, a 2010 report by the Council of Greater City Schools, which is a coalition of 65 of the nation's largest schools, indicated that "[b]lack males continue to perform lower than their peers throughout the country on almost every indicator."[32] Once again, our educational system has failed to identify and address the causes for the differential between white and African-American students, and within the subgroup of African-American boys and girls. African-American male students as a subgroup lag behind in academic achievement of all other students.

African-American students' test scores tend to be lower than white students' proficiency tests from kindergarten through high school. Since *Brown*, the gap between African-American students and whites has narrowed, but the differential between the gaps is still very prevalent.

As public schools resegregated, African-American students and other minorities remain in poorly funded, dilapidated school buildings, and are taught with outdated books and by less experienced teachers. Such conditions were similar to the pre-*Brown* period. The failure on the part

DOI: 10.1057/9781137408433.0006

of school districts to provide adequate resources and a positive learning environment may negatively impact minority students' academic achievement.

The use of standardized assessment and proficiency tests by school systems negatively impacts minority students' graduation rate, promotions, and placement. Where standardized tests have been challenged in court, courts have given deference to the states' educational policies. Despite this deference, courts recognize that state school systems have had a long history of discriminating against minority students. It is ironic that states which have historically discriminated against African-American students, by intentionally providing inferior educational opportunities, can now legally design standardized tests based on a system which has not corrected its past discriminatory acts.

3.1.7   The negative impact of sports in schools

The overemphasis of sports in the African-American community lessens the motivation of African-American males to strive for excellence in academia. A disproportionate number of young African-American males believe that playing sports will lead them to a professional sports contract. Consequently, their focus is not on making the honor roll or the debate team but the varsity basketball or football teams. Sadly, African-American males cling to the hope of playing professional sports after high school; however, the odds of playing professional sports are extremely remote. Supporters of sports programs in school will often point to success stories of African-American males who were inspired to stay in school because of their participation in sports. However, far too many African-American males who fail to maintain their "star status" are at the bottom of the academic scale. In addition, African-American male students who are not athletes also succumb to strive for mediocre grades. The preferential treatment that athletes receive lessens their motivation to achieve academically. Unfortunately, those few who go on to play collegiate sports maintain their "star status" until the season is over or until they can no longer play because of academic troubles or physical inability. A disproportionate number of African-American males who play collegiate sports fail to graduate from college, especially at NCAA Division I schools.[33]

African-American male athletes who are highly skilled are intensely worshipped, idolized, and praised by other students, teachers, alumni, and the press. On the contrary, African-American male students, who are not super-jocks, are ignored, invisible, and stereotyped.

The Supreme Court's ruling in *Brown* mandating equal and quality education for students regardless of their race has long been forgotten or ignored by state legislators who refuse to provide adequate funding for public schools. Since the *Brown* decision, all states ended the legal mandate to educate African-American and white students separately. Nevertheless, a majority of schools remain severely underfunded and segregated, with African-American males further segregated within these schools. The former Governor of Alabama George Wallace's infamous statement, "segregation now, segregation forever," correctly describes the current status of public schools in America. Thus, African-American students, African-American males in particular, are systematically denied educational opportunities.

There is no one solution to enhancing educational opportunities for African-American males. There must be holistic solutions developed at the national, state, and local levels of government. This includes the involvement of black parents, community organizations, and even the black church. Moreover, black parents must be both legally and morally accountable for the education of their sons. The burden of educating black boys cannot and should not be placed solely on teachers.

It appears that many black parents today have lost this urgency somewhere between fighting for school integration, instead of quality of education, placing too much emphasis on the playing of sports, and allowing overindulgence in the elements of pop culture. Failing to address this urgency directly impacts the employability and likelihood of criminal activity, and quality of life for young African-American male students will continue to struggle in a nation without an education. As the *Brown* decision has taught us, there must not be total reliance on the legal system to cure this problem. The African-American community should explore how to change and expand the culture of African-American males by partnering with school administrators to develop plans that devalue sports among African-American males and develop programs which emphasize academics.

States should pass laws that mandate parental accountability in the education of their children. School systems should develop alternatives to suspension and expulsion of students, develop alternative programs to reduce the number of African-American males in special education classes, and increase the number of African-American male teachers in

DOI: 10.1057/9781137408433.0006

secondary schools. Colleges and universities should develop affirmative action programs that are designed specifically to recruit, admit, and retain African-American males. Every school district should conduct an extensive study of the status of African-American male students at all stages of education.

Unless public school systems take an aggressive role in planning, developing, and implementing educational systems that meet the needs of all students, especially African-American males, the dream about which Martin Luther King spoke of and the decision in *Brown* is forever deferred.

3.2   Employment disparities and discrimination

3.2.1   Unemployment and underemployment of African-American males

The rate of unemployment and underemployment for African-American males has continued to worsen during the past four decades, with no indication that the trend will improve in the near future. A recent labor report states that unemployment indicators for Africa-Americans 16–19 years were approximately 31% for 2013, whereas the annual unemployment indicators for whites 16–19 years were approximately 21%. For African-American men 20 years and over, the unemployment indicators were 14% in 2013, whereas the annual unemployment indicators for white men were approximately 7% in 2013.[34] In major urban communities, the unemployment rate for African-American males is deplorable. For example, Montgomery County (Maryland) reports that in 2011, "nearly half of black male teens (47%) were unemployed."[35] A study by the University of California, Berkley, reports that in August 2012, the unemployment rate for black male teens between the ages of 16 and 19 was approximately 45%.[36] A 2010 study by the Community Service Society reports that "only one in four" African-American men between the ages of 16 and 24 years "had a job during the period from January 2009 to 2010."[37] Generations of African-American males across this country are unemployed, and unskilled; thus, they will never have an opportunity to enjoy the economic status of middle class citizens.

There are a number of factors that negatively impact the employability and status of African-American males in the workplace.[38] Debilitating factors such as the change from an industrial economy to a service-oriented economy,[39] recessionary periods,[40] the movement of blue collar and manufacturing jobs from urban inner cities to suburbs[41] or out of the country,[42] the elimination of semiskilled and unskilled occupations,[43] the influx of immigrants willing to accept jobs traditionally filled by African-American males, and a lack of education and training[44] have all proven to be direct causes of unemployment of African-American males, especially young African-American males.[45] In addition to these factors, having a criminal record will most likely result in being rejected for employment.

Disparities in wages, promotional opportunities, and other terms and conditions of employment between African-American and white males continue to widen. For example, the Economic Policy Institute reports that "in 2008 black men earned only 71% of what white men earned. The median hourly wage for black male full-time workers was $14.90; for comparable white workers it was $20.84."[46] A number of factors directly or indirectly cause the disparities between black and white males. For example, more employment opportunities are given to white males who reside in the suburbs than black males who reside in deteriorating urban areas. Other factors include the lack of education and marketable skills and employment discrimination.

Frederick Douglass predicted more than a century ago that:

> The old avocations, by which colored men obtained a livelihood, are rapidly unceasingly and inevitably passing into other hands; every hour sees the black man elbowed out of employment...It is evident, painfully evident to every reflecting mind, that the means of living, for colored men, are becoming more and more precarious and limited. Employment and callings, formerly monopolized by us, are so no longer.[47]

During the 1980s, African-American workers bore a relatively heavier burden of widespread job displacement because of the industries and occupations in which they were concentrated. They also were less likely to be rehired and were out of work longer. Similarly, the recession starting in 2009 disproportionally impacted African-Americans, particularly African-American males.[48]

3.2.2 Employment discrimination against African-American males

African-American males are generally impacted by other discriminatory factors.[49] These additional discriminatory factors have resulted in

DOI: 10.1057/9781137408433.0006

African-American males being intentionally and systematically denied employment and advancement opportunities.[50] Congress has promulgated a number of federal laws and regulations to prohibit employment discrimination directed at African-American males and other groups who have been historically discriminated against.[51] The judicial system's effectiveness and impartial enforcement of these laws to ensure equal employment opportunities for African-American males is still at issue.

Discrimination directed at African-American males appears to occur at all stages of the employment process: recruitment and initial interviewing, testing, grooming requirements, and job requirements. Discrimination directed at African-American males appears to be widespread, especially at the initial hiring stage. The use of employment "testers" has shown that some employers have a pattern and practice of discriminating against minorities, particularly African-American males. For example, the Fair Employment Council of Greater Washington ("FEC") and the Urban Institute used employment testing to reveal how employers systematically discriminated against qualified African-American male applicants. In both cases, African-American males were matched with white male applicants who had similar education, demeanor, and experience. Both groups of "testers" were trained to give the same responses to questions during the interview. In almost every contact with an employer by the "testers," the white male "testers" were given the job, treated more favorably, encouraged to apply for jobs with the employer, or offered a higher level job. Nevertheless, employers generally assert that if they could find "one" who was qualified, an African-American male would be hired.

The FEC audit established that BMC Marketing Corporation and Snelling treated white male applicants more favorably than the African-American male applicants, even though they had basically the same education, experience, and demeanor. FEC sued the above employers under Title VII and other federal and state laws seeking a declaratory judgment, permanent injunctive relief, and damages. The defendants filed a motion to dismiss the claims because the plaintiffs lacked standing to pursue such claims. The district court held that the testers had standing to sue under Title VII.[52]

The Urban Institute conducted a study of hiring practices of employers in Chicago and Washington, D.C., during the summer of 1990. The hiring audits examined how young black males were treated when applying for entry-level jobs in comparison with young white males with similar characteristics, education, and experience. The audit concluded that black males were unfavorably treated 20% of the time, whereas white males received unfavorable treatment 7% of the time when they were seeking the same jobs.[53]

These two employment audits illustrate that when employers have an opportunity to hire qualified African-American males, they still rely on stereotypical biases to deny African-American males employment. Many of these biases are related to how our justice system treats African-American males as guilty until proven innocent. This same negative predisposition influences employment decisions. It is almost as though the justice system has sanctioned such conduct. African-American males who reside in the inner city are often victims of employment discrimination based upon stereotypical racial biases.[54] There is also evidence that black males are treated adversely because of a combination of their race (black) and sex (male).[55] The courts, however, have not readily embraced this legal theory.[56]

African-American males are also targets for racial harassment[57] on the job and typically receive more severe disciplinary actions than white males for the same or similar infractions.[58] After the passage of Title VII of Civil Rights Act of 1964, the Supreme Court issued a number of favorable employment discrimination decisions where African-American males were either the plaintiff or directly benefited from the decision. The Court interpreted Title VII to prohibit employers from implementing employment policies and practices that, although neutral on their face, had a disparate impact on minorities, particularly African-American males.[59] The Supreme Court has also upheld affirmative action programs designed to ensure the employment and upward mobility of African-American males.[60] Very early on, the Court developed a flexible model for establishing a prima facie case of employment discrimination.[61] Again, the plaintiff was an African-American male.

As the Supreme Court became more conservative during the second half of the 1990s and into the 2000s, courts retreated from its posture of liberally interpreting Title VII in order to eradicate all vestiges of employment discrimination. Instead, the Court restricted the interpretation of Title VII, and has thus made it more difficult for minorities to bring disparate impact cases[62] and in individual disparate treatment cases.[63]

Even college-educated African-American males cannot shield themselves from stereotypical biases; they, too, face intentional discrimination

DOI: 10.1057/9781137408433.0006

in the workplace. For example, in *Barbour v. Merrill*,[64] an African-American male with extensive experience and master's degree related to the job was denied a position which was given to a white male with no degree and less experience. Similarly, in *Ayissi-Etoh v. Fannie Mae*,[65] an African-American male auditor alleged that he inquired of his supervisor why unlike others he did not get a pay increase after being promoted. The supervisor stated, "[f]or a young black man smart like you, we are happy to have your expertise; I think I'm already paying you a lot of money." The court determined that the term "young black man" alone was evidence of employment discrimination and he should be able to present the issue to a jury.[66]

Employers also intentionally exclude African-American males from senior-level positions and positions where they have contact with the public because of perceived and actual consumer prejudice directed at African-American males.

When African-American males are employed they are more likely to be suspended or terminated than white male employees who are involved in the same or similar infractions. A federal government study of the discharge rates of minority and nonminority employees in federal agencies revealed that the discharge rate for minorities, particularly African-American males, exceeded all other groups. In almost every type of discharge, for example, performance removals, termination during probation, minority males' rate of discharge doubled the rate of nonminority males. The disparity rate occurred in all regions of the country, as well as in all occupational categories.

In *Sims v. Montgomery County Comm'n*,[67] the court held that the defendant's policy of avoiding the assignment of white female police officers and African-American male police officers to share patrol cars is so overtly and clearly demeaning to African-Americans that it can only be characterized as racial harassment. Similarly, in *Davis v. Monsanto Chem. Co.*,[68] two African-American male employees alleged that a hostile work environment was created when racial slurs were directed at them, derogatory racial graffiti was written on the bathroom walls, and a safety poster was defamed to depict an African-American man as an incompetent worker. All of the above cases represent the type of disparate treatment and harassment that African-American males have alleged they experienced from white male supervisors and coworkers. These white supervisors and coworkers specifically directed their hostility at African-American males because of their hatred of African-American males. Typically, such

DOI: 10.1057/9781137408433.0006

intense hatred and hostility is not directed at African-American females; however, they are also racially harassed in the workplace. This is not to marginalize their experience but to suggest that their experiences may be different from that of African-American males.[69] African-American males are also systematically denied work assignments which could lead to upward mobility.[70]

They are also assigned the less desirable duties in organizations, more often accused of and terminated for sexual harassment, monitored more closely, receive lower performance evaluations, and are continuously confronted with hostility in the workplace. A further cause of unemployment, underemployment, and discrimination against African-American males stems from stereotypical biases about African-American male workers. These stereotypical biases result in exclusion from employment opportunities. African-American males who face employment discrimination will find it extremely difficult to prove the existence of discrimination in court, or even with administrative agencies.

3.2.3   The impact of criminal records on employment of African-American males

I often ask my law students what they would do if they had a criminal record which prohibited them from finding employment, getting a student loan or grants, housing, and the means to take care of one's family. African-American males who have served their prison term and seek to become law-abiding citizens may quickly find their employment opportunities more scarce. They may find going back to the crime of selling drugs on the corner as the only option they have to survive. Ultimately they will return to prison and the cycle starts again. It is called as recidivism. This is not to condone such conduct but only to disclose the reality that African-American males face every day. How should the issue of criminal records be addressed to balance the interest of public employers, and individuals with criminal records?

According to the U.S. Justice Department of Statistics on prisoners in State and Federal Correctional facilities, more than half a million of African-American males are incarcerated every year. Once they are released from incarceration they will be branded for life as an individual with a criminal record. African-American males who have arrest records may also face employment discrimination. A study of arrest records from 1997 to 2008 determined that "about 49% of African-American

DOI: 10.1057/9781137408433.0006

males have been arrested" and "the risk of arrest by age of 23 was 30%."[71] It will be extremely difficult to find employment opportunities because of their criminal record.

African-American males who have criminal records are forever branded as second-class citizens. They will be relegated to temporary low-paying jobs with little hope of gaining full employment or promotional opportunities. Indeed, having a criminal record will undoubtedly make it extremely difficult to find employment, housing, credit, in some states the right to vote in elections, and in many jurisdictions to get a professional license, such as a barber license.[72] If an African-American male with a criminal record can find employment, they are hired in "day jobs" and temporary employment, paid less than minimal wages, or paid in cash under the table by employers.

These types of jobs provide limited job security, benefits, retirement plans, or protections by federal employment laws. Moreover, they face humiliation and blatant harassment by unscrupulous employers who recognize that employees with criminal records will not complain because their opportunity for employment elsewhere is extremely limited.

States must pass legislation that restricts employers from implementing broad employment policies that deny individuals with criminal record an opportunity to obtain employment. Moreover, the aggressive enforcement of discrimination laws by the U.S. Equal Employment Commission (EEOC) is crucial. In 2012, the EEOC issued policy guidelines on how an employer may use criminal records to make employment decisions that could violate Title VII of the Civil Rights Act.[73] The Guidelines set forth guidance to employers on how to avoid a violation of Title VII. The EEOC explained that federal laws could be violated if an employer treats a white male who has a criminal record more favorably than an African-American male with a criminal record. Interestingly, a study on the impact of race and criminal records on an applicant's ability to get a job concludes that African-American males are more disadvantaged than white male applicants. The study revealed that employers were more likely to hire a white male with a criminal record than an African-American male, when their criminal history is very similar.[74]

The EEOC has taken an aggressive approach to end the blanket exclusion of all ex-felons from employment in any job with an employer. The EEOC filed suit against BMW for failing to meet the business necessity test for having a broad no-hire policy of individuals with a criminal record. Not all employers have welcomed the EEOC's enforcement policy. In 2014, Texas, for example, brought a suit seeking a declaratory judgment regarding the state prohibition of hiring ex-felons in any position in a number of state agencies. The Texas Attorney General alleges the EEOC policy is unreasonable.[75]

African-American males with a criminal record will be required to disclose the fact they have a conviction record each and every time they apply for a position. Almost automatically, the employer will deny them a job because of the company's policy on not hiring individuals with convictions. Though neutral on its face, this policy could violate Title VII, based on the theory of disparate impact.[76] Employers, however, will have an opportunity to raise a business necessity affirmative defense. The EEOC has indicated that discrimination could be unintentional where an employer implements a neutral policy of not hiring anyone with a criminal record, regardless of the offense. African-American males may be disproportionately impacted unless the employer can justify the policy-based business necessity, the employer may be liable.

The enforcement of the EEOC policy on criminal records and on exclusionary policies will open the door for thousands of African-American males who have paid their debt to society to find and maintain meaningful employment. Because employers only have to show there is a manifest relationship between the policy and performance of the job, it will be difficult for plaintiff to win such claims.

3.3   Voting disenfranchisement of African-American males

According to the Sentencing Project, approximately two million African-Americans' ability to vote in this country has been abridged temporarily or permanently.[77] The Sentencing Project also projected "1 of every 13 African-American of voting age is disenfranchised, a rate more than four times greater than non-African-Americans."[78] States have promulgated voting laws which prohibit prisoners, parolees, and ex-felons from voting. As a result of African-American males being disproportionately incarcerated, they will mostly be impacted by disenfranchisement laws.[79] State disenfranchisement laws represent the new poll tax, literacy test, grandfather clause, and property ownership requirements which were previously used to exclude African-Americans from exercising their right to vote.

DOI: 10.1057/9781137408433.0006

The exclusionary voting policies of states were exposed in the 2000 presidential election, when it was determined that more than 200,000 African-American males of voting age in Florida were denied the opportunity to vote.[80] Extensive legal scholarship has been published on how voter disenfranchisement laws are having a devastating impact on African-American males. However, states have been slow to modify their disenfranchisement statutes to ensure that all their citizens have the opportunity to vote as guaranteed by the Constitution and the Voting Rights Act. A number of states have established procedures to re-enfranchise ex-felons; however, the processes are often highly complicated or too costly for ex-felons to pursue. The courts have been reluctant to find the process of restoring voting rights, even if convoluting, a violation of the Constitution. In denying a claim that Virginia's process was unconstitutional, the court stated in *El-Amin v. McDonnell* that:

> It is true that Virginia is one of only four states—along with Florida, Iowa, and Kentucky—that require individual felons to file actual applications to have their voting rights restored. In the vast majority of states, once a felon completes his or her imprisonment and any period of parole and/or probation, that person's voting rights automatically return. That said, if the only differences between the Commonwealth and a sizeable group of other states are that a person in Virginia must meet certain basic and eminently reasonable criteria for eligibility, and file a straightforward petition for reinstatement, this Court cannot conclude that its application process renders its felon disenfranchisement provision cruel and unusual.[81]

There have been a number of unsuccessful constitutional challenges of state felon's disenfranchisement laws.[82] In *Wesley v. Collins*,[83] an African-American male alleged that Tennessee's disenfranchisement law violated Section 2 of the Voting Rights Act of 1965.[84] The court denied there was a violation of the Act. The Court stated:

> That the [state] may disqualify convicted felons from voting public without unlawfully interfering with equal opportunity of blacks to participate in the political process and to elect representatives of their choice.[85]

In the State of Alabama, the Circuit Court of Jefferson County held in *Gooden v. Worley*[86] that Alabama law denying the right to vote to citizens convicted of "moral turpitude" was void until the legislation decided what crimes fall under this definition. The ruling may provide felons an opportunity the right to vote. Similarly, the State of Washington's disenfranchisement and restoration policies were challenged by racial

DOI: 10.1057/9781137408433.0006

minorities in *Farrakham v. Gregoire.*[87] Even though there was compelling evidence that there was a "racial bias in Washington's criminal justice system" which negatively impacted ex-felons' right to vote, the Court held that the State of Washington's felon disenfranchisement law did not violate §2 of the Voting Rights Act.[88]

The Supreme Court in *Richardson v. Ramirez*[89] held there were no Fourteenth Amendment limitations on state promulgating disenfranchisement laws.[90] Justice Marshall in a dissenting opinion stated:

> It is doubtful…whether the state can demonstrate either a compelling or rational policy interest in denying former felons the right to vote. The individuals involved in the present case are persons who have fully paid their debt to society. They are as much affected by the actions of government as any other citizens, and have as much of a right to participate in governmental decision-making. Furthermore, the denial of the right to vote to such persons is a hindrance to the efforts of society to rehabilitate former felons and convert them into law-abiding and productive citizens.[91]

A majority of states prohibit individuals who are in prison, on probation, and on parole from voting. During the past decade, a number of states have relaxed the prohibition of ex-felons from voting for life. However, Florida, Kentucky, and Virginia still disenfranchise more than 20% of African-Americans from voting, even though African-American males are disproportionately harmed by such laws. The Sentencing Project has determined that as of 2014, twelve jurisdictions including Alabama, Arizona, Delaware, Florida, Iowa, Kentucky, Mississippi, Nebraska, Nevada, Tennessee, Virginia, Wyoming have laws which disenfranchise ex-felons, including individuals who are inmates, parolees, and probationers.[92]

Interestingly, the states that disenfranchise ex-felons for life are located in the South. The greatest concentrations of slaves were also located in the South who were also denied the right to vote. Moreover, the southern states have the highest percentage of African-American males incarcerated in the country.[93]

After Reconstruction, Southern states, in particular, and other states as well, but less restrictive passed disenfranchisement voting laws to control and limit blacks the right to vote.[94] For example, Georgia restricts African-American males from voting if they are in prison or on probation or parole and this has resulted in approximately 65,000 African-American males being denied the opportunity to vote.[95] The present-day effect on African-American voters and particularly African-American

DOI: 10.1057/9781137408433.0006

male voters is still prevalent. For example, in Virginia,[96] it is estimated that 243,000 African-Americans are unable to vote: 137,000 in Alabama,[97] 520,000 in Florida,[98] 156,000 in Texas,[99] and 107,000 in Mississippi.[100] African-American males continue to face state restrictions on their right to vote.

The Voting Rights Act of 1965 was passed to ensure all Americans could vote without facing discrimination or other barriers to keep them from voting. This Act not only opened the door for African-American males to freely vote but all Americans. However, in 2013, the Supreme Court in *Shelby County v. Holder*[101] struck down the preclearance provision in Section 5 of the Act. This provision prevented certain jurisdictions from making changes to their voting practice until reviewed and approved by the Justice Department. The preclearance provision prevented certain jurisdictions from implementing discriminatory voting procedures. This decision will undoubtedly open the door for states, particularly in the South, to unilaterally make changes in voting procedures and qualifications which could further limit the rights of African-Americans to vote.

State disenfranchisement laws are not limited to just voting but also to employment,[102] housing, and the opportunity to serve on a federal jury. As stated earlier, many employers have policies which prohibit the employment of individuals with criminal records.[103] Again, African-American males are adversely impacted by such laws and policies, similar to periods of slavery and past reconstruction. The mass numbers of African-American males who are incarcerated will face the collateral effect of imprisonment once they are released and seek to exercise their Constitutional rights.[104]

As a result of political pressures from the press and the public and civil rights organizations, states have made some prorogues in modifying their disenfranchisement laws to allow ex-felons and other individuals under control of the corrections system. The federal government has also strongly encouraged states to grant ex-felons the right to vote. In early 2014, Attorney General Eric Holder, in a speech in Washington, D.C., stated:

> It's time to fundamentally reconsider laws that permanently disenfranchise people who are no longer under federal or state supervision. These restrictions are not only unnecessary and unjust, they are also counter-productive. By perpetuating the stigma and isolation imposed on formerly incarcerated individuals, these laws increase the likelihood they will commit future crimes.[115]

Without the right to vote, African-American males are devalued by the various political systems which promulgate policies that disproportionately impact their Constitutional rights.[106] Re-enfranchising African-American males will empower them to actively participate in our system of democracy.[107] A failure to do so revert African-American males to second-class citizens or, even worse, subordinates than to a system of *de facto* slavery.

State voting laws which restrict the rights of felons to vote have resulted in the subordination of African-American males of a very basic constitutional right, the right to vote. The struggle continues for African-American males to exercise their constitutional right to vote without restrictions or barriers.

The massive disenfranchisement of African-American males in this country further isolates them from the general public. The isolation of African-American males is already evident in employment and education. The denial of voting further subordinates their status socially, economically, and politically.

3.4 Racial disparity in health and health care

The overall health of African-American males, young and old, poor or middle class, continues to deteriorate. The cause for the health risk African-Americans face is varied. Where most Americans expect to die from natural causes or medical illnesses, for young African-American males they expect to be a victim of a homicide or a violent crime. Eighty-five percent of African-American males who are victims of homicide are young and between the ages of 17 and 29 years.[108] The probability of an African-American male being murdered during his lifetime is approximately 42 per 1000, whereas the probability for white males is 6 per 1000.[109]

The U.S. Department of Justice reports that:

▸ Between 1980 and 2008, young adult black males had the highest offending rate compared to offenders in other racial and sex categories.
▸ The offending rate for black male young adults remained more than double the rate of black male teens.
▸ Black males were disproportionately represented as both homicide victims and offenders.[110]

DOI: 10.1057/9781137408433.0006

The homicide rates reflect simple but depressing conclusions. African-American males kill other black males in large number, starting at age 14 years.[111] Because of the easy access to guns, African-American males most likely use a firearm to commit crimes.[112]

The life expectancy of African-American males has continued to decline, whereas for white males it has increased. A 1996 study of mortality rate among African-Americans and whites in the United States determined that an African-American male living in Harlem had a less likely chance to reach age 65 years than a person who lived in Bangladesh, one of the poorest countries in the world.[113] Approximately, twenty years later, the life expectancy for African-American males is still lower than any other group. For example, in 2009, the life expectancy for African-American males was 71.1 years, while for white males it was 76.4 years.[114] The life expectancy continues to improve but still negatively by HIV infection and homicide. Other studies indicate that African-American males have a shorter life expectancy than whites because of educational differences.[115] There is a correlation between education attainment and life expectancy. Clearly, based on the low high school and college graduation rates of African-American males, their life expectancy will continue to be less than that of white males.

Aside from the issue of homicide, national health statistics report that the mortality among African-American males is substantially higher than that for white males. The probability of an African-American male dying between the ages of 15 and 60 years is 30.3%, whereas white males have a probability of 16%. There are further reports that African-American males disproportionately die from injuries such as drowning, pedestrian mishaps, and residential fires.

A major health crisis for African-American males is the various forms of cancer. The National Cancer Institute reports that African-American males have the highest rate of prostate cancer than any other group. Prostate cancer "is the second most fatal cancer among black men, after lung cancer." Indeed, according to the American Cancer Society, "the death rate for all cancers combined ... is 32% higher for African-American men."[116] However, there is evidence that smoking-related cancers have decreased among African-American males, but they continue to have the highest percent of adults who are current cigarette smokers.[117] This may be the reason that that "African American men are 37 percent more likely to develop lung cancer than white men."[118] According to the Center for Disease Control and Prevention (CDC), "African-American men have

DOI: 10.1057/9781137408433.0006

the highest rate of lung cancer in the Unites States."[119] The incidence rate for colorectal cancer among Africa-American men now surpasses that of white men.[120] Much of the health problems that African-American males are inflicted with are the direct result of unhealthy eating habits, a lack of physical exercise, and smoking.

AIDS has also had a devastating impact on the lives of Africa-American males. The CDC reports that African-American men have the highest rate of AIDS exposure than any other group, especially in urban areas. Specifically, the CDC reports that:

> African-American men accounted for 43% of HIV cases diagnosed among men in 2011. A majority (72%) of African-American men with HIV contracted the disease by male to male contact.[121]

These numbers clearly support the conclusion that African-American men are facing a HIV health crisis. The CDC also has determined that "unless the course of the epidemic changes, at some point in their lifetime, an estimated 1 in 16 black men and 1 in 32 black women will be diagnosed with HIV infection."[122] Further efforts are needed to educate the African-American communities on the AIDS crisis. Specifically designed educational programs for African-American males on how to protect them from contacting HIV and how to get appropriate medical attention if infected are needed. There still exist a great amount of stigma on HIV/AIDS in the African-American community, thus infected minorities may delay in getting appropriate health care out of fear that their community will become aware of their condition. Moreover, there must be a greater effort for HIV testing and prevention programs that are specifically designed to educate members of the African-American community.

The suicide rate of white males still outnumbers African-American males who commit suicide. White males who commit suicide are typically retired, 65 and older. African-American males who commit suicide are typically between 25 and 34 years and unable to continually face everyday stresses, such as facing racism on the job, repeatedly being rejected when applying for a job, and even when enjoying the normal pleasures of shopping, buying a home, or vacationing.[123]

Poverty is probably the primary reason for the deteriorating health of African-American males. Some studies suggest that individuals living below the poverty level are more likely to develop health problems. African-Americans, particularly African-American males, are

DOI: 10.1057/9781137408433.0006

disproportionately at or below the poverty level. For example, the U.S. Census Bureau reported that in 2012, 12.8% of whites were at the poverty level, whereas 27.6 of African-Americans were at that level.[124]

Racism directed at African-American males and being unemployment are two major underlying causes of stress, hypertension, and suicide. Hypertension has also disproportionately affected the health of African-American males. Studies have suggested that this is a result of the rage that Black males and other minorities must suppress to attempt acceptance by white Americans.[125]

As discussed in earlier chapters, African-American males face racism in employment, education, and how they are treated by law enforcement officials. Racism is just a part of their everyday life experiences. These factors will undoubtedly affect their mental and physical health.[126] The hospitalization of African-American males as patients in mental health facilities has increased substantially. This is an indication that African-American males are facing a life of adversities that is negatively impacting their mental health. Moreover, a study on the impact that childhood adversity has on the health of African-American males determined that it can have a negative impact on their physical and mental health as an adult.[127] White males are less impacted by adversity they faced as a child.

The poor health condition of African-Americans, particularly males, may be caused in part because of poor health care services and access to services. The 2012 *National Healthcare Disparities Report*[128] determined that African-Americans face more barriers to access to health care than whites, and that the disparity is getting worse not better. For example, a stroke which may cause death may be misdiagnosed in an African-American male.[129] There is also evidence that there is racial disparity between whites and African-Americans in receiving alcohol treatment.[130]

Recognizing there is still disparity in health care services for African-Americans, the National Institute on Drug Abuse has incorporated into their strategic plan to expand research on appropriate "prevention, treatment and health services" for African-Americans and ethnic communities.[131] Racial disparities in health care services have been well documented by a number of leading health care experts. They all agree that race is a factor in the quality of health services that are provided.[132]

Until access to health care services and the quality of services improve, the health of African-American males will continue to be at risk. An increased number of African-American male doctors in underserved

DOI: 10.1057/9781137408433.0006

minority communities and expanded research on specific heath issues facing African-American males would be a step in the right direction. Improving the ability of heath care professionals to communicate effectively with African-American males regarding their heath is also urgently needed. It is hoped that with the passage of the Affordable Care Act that requires all Americans to have health care coverage, African-American males will receive much needed health services.

Notes

1   347 U.S. 483 (1954).

2   Sara Ganim, *Some College Athletes Play Like Adults, Read Like 5th-Grader*, CNN. com. (January 8, 2014, 1:05 PM), *available at* http://cpf.cleanprint.net/cpf?a ction=printer&filePrint&key=cnn&key=http%3A%2f (last visited May 28, 2014).

3   *Schott Foundation for Public Education, the Urgency of Now, the Schott 50 State on Public Education and Black Males* (2012), *available* at http://www. schottfoundation.org/publications-reports/.

4   *See*, National Center of Education Statistics (2012), *available at* http://neces. ed.gov/programs/digest/d13/tables/dt13 218.70.asp.

5   *U.S. Census Bureau, Statistical Abstract of the United States* (2012), *available at* http://wwcensus.gov/population/www/socfemp/school.html.

6   Stephanie Ewert, Bryan Sykes, & Becky Pettit, *The Degree of Disadvantage: Incarceration and Inequality in Education* (February 12, 2010), *available at* http://paa2010.princeton.edu/papers/101763.

7   *U.S. Census Bureau, Statistical Abstract of the United States, College Enrollment by Sex, Age, Race, and Hispanic Origin 1980–2009, available at* http:www.census. gov/population/www/socdemo/school.html.

8   *U.S. Department of Education Office of Civil Rights, Civil Rights Data Collection; Data Snapshot: School Discipline* (March 2014), *available at* www.ocrdata.edu. gov (last visited May 28, 2014).

9   John Mays, *Nashville Middle Schools Suspend 50 Percent of Black Boys, African America. Org* (June 4, 2010), *available at* http://www.africanamerica.org/topic/ nashville-middle-schools-suspend-50-percent-of-black-boys.

10 *Urban Strategies Council, African American Male Achievement Initiative: A Close Look at Suspensions of African American Males in Ousd, 2010–2011, 21* (May 2012), *available at* urbanstrategies.org/aamai/ . . . /AAMA_OUSD_ SuspensionAnalysis.pdf.

11 Daniel J. Losen & Russell J. Skiba, *University of California, The Civil Rights Project, Suspended Education Urban Middle Schools in Crisis* (2010), *available at* civilrightsproject.ucla.edu (last visited May 28, 2014).

DOI: 10.1057/9781137408433.0006

12 *U.S. Department of Education. National Center for Education Statistics, Status and Trends in the Education of Blacks* (September 2003), *available at* nces.ed.gov/pubs2003/2003034.pdf.

13 *See*, Daniel J. Losen & Russell J. Skib, *supra* note 11. Also *see*, Daniel J. Losen & Jonathan Gillespie, *Opportunities Suspended: The Disparate Impact of Disciplinary Exclusion from School* (August 7, 2012), *available at* http://escholarship.org/uc/item/3g36n0c3.(last visited May 28, 2012).

14 Daniel J. Losen & Tia Elena Martinez, *Out of School & Off Track, The Center for Civil Rights Remedies* (April 8, 2013), *available at* http://civilrightsproject.ucla.edu/resources/projects/center-for-civil-rights-remedies/school-to-prison-folder/federal-reports/out-of-school-and-off-track-the-overuse-of-suspensions-in-american-middle-and-high-schools.

15 376 F. Supp. 1330 (N.D. Tex. 1974).

16 *See*, Tom Rudd, *Kirwan Institute Issue Brief, Racial Disproportionality in School Discipline, Implicit Bias is Heavily Implicated* (February 2014) (includes a number of studies on the disproportionality of African-American males who were suspended) (last visited May 28, 2014).

17 251 F.3d 662, 2001 U.S. App. LEXIS 10593 (7th Cir. Ill. 2001).

18 2000 U.S. Dist. LEXIS 21772, 2000 WL 33680483 (M.D. Ala. August 30, 2000).

19 *See*, Ivory A. Toldson, Tyne Mcgee, & Brianna P. Lemmons, *Reducing Suspensions by Improving Academic Engagement among School Age Black Males* (April 6, 2013), *available at* http://civilrightsproject.ucla.edu/resources/projects/center-for-civil-rights-remedies/school-to-prison-folder/state-reports/copy3_of_dignity-disparity-and-desistance-effective-restorative-justice-strategies-to-plug-the-201cschool-to-prison-pipeline/toldson-reducing-suspension-ccrr-conf-2013.pdf (last visited May 28, 2014).

20 *U.S. Department of Justice Civil Rights, Nondiscriminatory Administration of School Discipline* (January 8, 2014), *available at* http://www.justice.gov/crt/about/edu/documents/dcl.pdf.

21 299 F.Supp. 2d 1340 (M.D. Ga. 2004); Also see, George W. Moore & John R. Slate, *Who's Talking the Advanced Placement Courses and How Are They Doing: A Statewide Two-Year Study, High School Journal, the University of North Carolina Press* (2008), 56–67, *available at* http://edukator.homestead.com/AP/Who_s_Taking_the_AP_Courses_and_How_Are_They_Doing.pdf.

22 City of Thomasville School District, 299 F. Supp 2d 1340 at 1356.

23 269 F. Supp. 401 (D. D.C. 1976).

24 246 F.3d 1073 (7th Cir. 2001).

25 *Id*. at 1081.

26 100 U.S. 303 (1879).

27 To address the exclusory practice, a task force was organized in Maryland. The taskforce proposed that "...that every public high school offers an

Advanced Placement (AP) program and that the prevalence of African-American males enrolled in AP reflects the demographics of the overall student population, *see Task Force on the Maryland's African-American Males* (December 2006), *available at* www.justicepolicy.org/uploads/ . . . / documents/blackmales2007.pdf

28 Jamila Codrington & Halford B. Fairchild, *The Association of Black Psychologists, Special Education and the Mis-Education of African American Children: A Call to Action* (February 13, 2012), *available at* http://www.abpsi. org/pdf/specialedpositionpaper021312.pdf (last visited May 28, 2014).

29 348 F. Supp. 866 (D.D.C. 1972).

30 343 F. Supp 1306 (N.D. Cal. 1972), *aff'd*, 502 F. Supp. 963 (9th Cir. 1974); 495 F.2d 926 (N.D. Cal. 1979), *aff'd*, 793 F.2d 969 (9th Cir. 1984).

31 506 F. Supp. 831 (N.D. Ill. 1980).

32 *Council of the Great City Schools, a Call for Change: The Social and Educational Factors Contributing to the Outcome of Black Males in Urban Schools* (October 2011), *available at* http//win.edweek.org/media/black_male_study.

33 See, Shaun Harper, *Black Men as College Athletes; The Real Win-Lose Record, The Chronicle of Higher Education, Commentary*, January 20, 2014, *available at* http://chronicle.com/article/Black-Men-as-College-Athletes-/144095/ (last visited May 28, 2014); Shaun R. Harper, Collin D. Williams Jr., & Horatio W. Blackman, *Black Male Student-Athletes and Racial Inequities in NCAA Division I College Sports*, 2013, *available at* http://www.gse.upenn.edu/equity/sites/ gse.upenn.edu.equity/files/publications/Harper_Williams_and_Blackman_ (2013).pdf (last visited May 28, 2014).

34 *U.S. Bureau of Labor Statistics, Employment Status of the Civilian Population by Race, Sex, and Age* (2013), *available at* http://www.bls.gov/news.release/empsit. to2.htm.

35 Elaine Bonner-Tompkins & Sue Richards, *Youth and Work in Montgomery County* (December 10, 2013), *available at* www.montgomerycountymd.gov/ OLO/ . . . /FullOLOReport2014-3.pdf (last visited May 28, 2014).

36 University of California Berkeley Center for Labor Research, *Annual Report: Black Employment and Unemployment in 2012* (February 2013), *available at* http:// laborcenter.berkeley.edu/press/release_feb13.shtml (last visited May 28, 2014.

37 Community Service Society, *Only One In Four Young Black Men In New York Has A Job, available at* http://www.cssny.org/publications/entry/ unemployment-in-new-york-cityDec2010 (last visited May 28, 2014).

38 *See generally Center for the Study of Social Policy, World without Work, causes and Consequences of Black Male Joblessness* (1994), *available at* http://www.cssp. org/publications/neighborhood-investment/world-without-work-causes-and-consequences-of-black-male-joblessness.pdf; Phillip Moss & Chris Tilly, *Why Black Men are Doing Worse in the Labor Market: A Review of Supply-Side & Demand-Side Explanations* (1991) (reporting how labor demand shifts, supply

DOI: 10.1057/9781137408433.0006

shifts, and institutional reformation in the labor market have negatively impacted African-American males in the labor market).

39   *See* Jared Bernstein. Where's the Payoff? The Gap Between Black Academic Progress & Economic Gains, *Econ. Policy Inst.*, 3, 40 (1995) (finding that the shift from well-paying jobs in manufacturing to low earning service jobs during the 1980s hurt African-American male workers).

40   *See The Recession and the Work Force: Hearing Before the Senate Comm. on Labor and Human Resources*, 102d Cong. 64–68 (1991) (testimony on America's recession and its effects on the work force, indicating that African-Americans suffer disproportionately high unemployment during recessions).

41   *See* Algernon Austin, *Transporting Black Men to Good Jobs*, posted October 5, 2012, *available at* http://www.epi.org/blog/transporting-black-men-good-jobs/;Thomas Hyclak & James Stewart, *A Note on the Relative Earnings of Central City Black Males*, 16 *J. Hum. Resources* 304 (1981).

42   Carol Stump, *Free Trade Area of the Americas*, 4 *J. Int'l L. & Prac.* 153, 169 (1995) (discussing how NAFTA has caused thousands of jobs to disappear, with the largest net affect on females and minorities).

43   *See generally* McKinley L. Blackburn et al., The Declining Position of Less Skilled American Men, *in A Future of Lousy Jobs?: The Changing Structure of U.S. Wages* (Gary Burtless ed., 1990).

44   *See Disadvantaged Youth Unemployment: Hearing Before the Subcomm. on Labor of the Senate Comm. on Labor and Human Resources*, 100th Cong. (1987) (discussing the lack of education, work experience and unemployment of inner-city minority youths); *U.S. Commission on Civil Rights, the Economic Progress of Black Men* 43 (1986) [hereinafter *Progress of Black Men*] (finding that racial differences in education can be a factor in racial differences in unemployment).

45   Jewelle T. Gibbs ed., *Young, Black, and Male in America: An Endangered Species* (1988). *See also* Bernstein, *supra* note 6, at 1–4, 7–8 (finding that the level of education for African-Americans, especially African-American males, has risen over the past thirty years, while their economic progress has fallen).

46   Andrea Orr, *Economic Policy Institute Why Do Black Men Earn Less?* (March 3, 2011), *available at* http://www.epi.org/publication/why-do_black_men_earn_less/ (last visited May 28, 2014).

47   Herbert Hill, *Black Labor and American Legal System* 12–13 (1977) (quoting Frederick Douglass).

48   *U.S. Department of Labor, the African-American Labor Force in the Recovery*, February 29, 2012, *available at* http://www.dol.gov/_sec/media/reports/blacklaborforce/; Lori G. Kletzer, *Job Displacement 1979–86: How Blacks Fared Relative to Whites*, 114 *Monthly Lab. Rev.* 17, 19 (July 1991). *See* generally, McKinley L. Blackburn, et al., The Declining Position of Less Skilled

DOI: 10.1057/9781137408433.0006

American Men, in *A Future of Lousy Jobs?: The Changing Structure of U.S. Wages* (Gary Burtless ed., 1990).

49   Darrick Hamilton et al., *Economic Policy Institute Whiter Jobs, Higher Wages, Occupational Segregation and the Lower Wages of Black Men* (2011), *available at* http://www.epi.org/pblication/whiter_jobs_higher_wages/; Stephen Nord & Yuan Ting, *Discrimination and the Unemployment Duration of White and Black Males, 26 Applied Econ.* 969, 977 (1994) (finding that the unemployment duration differential between African-American and white males is largely due to discrimination).

50   *See Lams v. General Waterworks Corp.*, 766 F.2d 386 (8th Cir. 1985) (finding that African-American males were systematically denied promotional opportunities on the presumption they preferred lower level positions, even though they showed an interest in being promoted); *Holsey v. Armour & Co.*, 743 F.2d 199 (4th Cir. 1984), *cert. denied*, 470 U.S. 1028 (1985) (upholding the district court=s finding that the company had engaged in a pattern of discrimination against African-American males on promotion and job assignments); Andrew M. Gill, *The Role of Discrimination In Determining Occupational Structure*, 42 Indus. & Lab. Rel. Rev. 610 (1989) (presenting statistical data which substantiate that employment discrimination is a reason why minorities and specifically African-American men are excluded from managerial, sales, clerical, and craft positions).

51   *See*, e.g., Title VII of the Civil Rights Act of 1964, 42 U.S.C. 2000e (1988).

52   *FEC v. BMC Marketing Corp.*, 829 F. Supp. 402, 407 (D.C. 1993), *modified*, 28 F.3d 1268 (D.C. Cir. 1994) (holding that the testers lacked standing). For a review of FEC's employment testing project, see Marc Bendick Jr. et al., *Fair Employment Council of Greater Washington Measuring Employment Discrimination Through Controlled Experiments* (1993).

53   Margery Turner et al., Opportunities Denied. OPPORTUNITIES Diminished: Discrimination In Hiring 1, *The Urban Inst.*, Rep. No. 91–9, (1991).

54   *Id.* at 3. Also see Devah Pager et al., *Race at Work: A Field Experiment of Discrimination in Low-Wage Labor Markets*, 2008, *available at* http://www.law.virginia.edu/pdf/workshops/0708/pager.pdf (used testers to determine the impact of criminal records on gaining employment).

55   *See* generally Note, *Invisible Man: Black and Male Under Title VII*, 104 Harv. L. Rev. 749 (1991).

56   D. Aaron Lacy, *The Most Endangered Title VII Plaintiff? Exponential Discrimination Against Black Males*, 86 Neb L. Rev. 552 (2008); Floyd D. Weatherspoon, *Remedying Employment Discrimination Against African-American Males: Stereotypical Biases Engender a Case of Race Plus Sex Discrimination*, 36 Washburn L. J. 23 (1996).

57   *Kimble v. Wis. Dep't of Workforce Dev.*, 690 F. Supp. 2d 765, 2010 U.S. Dist. LEXIS 16793 (E.D. Wis. 2010); *Taylor v. Local 32 E Service Employees Intern.*,

DOI: 10.1057/9781137408433.0006

Union, 286 F. Supp.2d 246 (S.D.N.Y. 2003); *McGinnis v. Ingram Equip. Co.*, 685 F. Supp. 224, 225–227 (N.D. Ala. 1988), *vacated*, 888 F.2d 109 (11th Cir. 1989), *vacated and reh'g en banc* granted, 895 F.2d 1303 (11th Cir. 1990).

58   Cf. Andrew Hacker, *Two Nations: Black and White, Separate, Hostile, Unequal* 117–18 (1992) ("[B]lacks must put in a lot more effort simply to satisfy the standards their employers set.").

59   *Griggs v. Duke Power Co.*, 401 U.S. 424, 430 (1971).

60   United Steelworkers of America, *AFL-CIO v. Weber*, 443 U.S. 193, 209 (1979).

61   *McDonnell Douglas Corp. v. Green*, 411 U.S. 792, 802 (1973).

62   *Ricci v. DeStefano*, 557 U.S.557 (2009).

63   *See St. Mary's Honor Ctr. v. Hicks*, 113 S. Ct. 2742 (1993).

64   *Barbour v. Merrill*, 48 F.3d 1270, 310 U.S. App. D.C. 419, 1995 U.S. App. LEXIS 4671, 67 Fair Empl. Prac. Cas. (BNA) 369, 31 Fed. R. Serv. 3d (Callaghan) 403 (D.C. Cir. 1995).

65   *Ayissi-Etoh v. Fannie Mae*, 712 F.3d 572, 404 U.S. App. D.C. 291, 2013 U.S. App. LEXIS 6870, 117 Fair Empl. Prac. Cas. (BNA) 1551, 2013 WL 1352239 (D.C. Cir. 2013).

66   *Ayissi-Etoh* at 575.

67   *Sims v. Montgomery County Comm'n*, 544 F. Supp. 420, 1982 U.S. Dist. LEXIS 15071, 33 Fair Empl. Prac. Cas. (BNA) 618 (M.D. Ala. 1982).

68   858 F.2d 345 (6th Cir. 1988), *cert. denied*, 490 U.S. 1110 (1989).

69   766 F. Supp. 1052 (M.D. Ala. 1991).

70   *See Steele v. Louisville & N.R. Co.*, 323 U.S. 192 (1944). For a discussion of the *Lewis* case, see Vicki Schultz and Stephen Petterson, *Race, Gender, Work, And Choice: An Empirical Study of the Lack of Interest Defense in Title VII Cases Challenging Job Segregation*, 59 U. Chi. L. Rev. 1073, 1152–1156 (1992).

71   Robert Brame et al., *Demographic Patterns of Cumulative Arrest Prevalence by Ages 18 and 23*, Crime & Delinquency (January 6, 2014), *available at* http://bit.ly/1dCuuRw (last visited May 28, 2014).

72   Michael Pinard, *Criminal Records, Race and Redemption*, 16 Leg. & Pub. Pol'y, 963 (2013) (provides a comprehensive review of the impact of criminal records on individuals to gain employment and to obtain housing, proposes a redemption model to remove criminal records from public access).

73   EEOC Enforcement Guidance No: N-915.002, *Consideration of Arrest and Conviction Records in Employment Decisions Under Title VII of the Civil Rights Act of 1964* (April 25, 2012), *available at* http://www.eeoc.gov/laws/guidance/arrest_conviction.cfm.

74   *See*, Devah Pager, Bruce Western, & Naomi Sugie, *Sequencing Disadvantage: Barriers to Employment Facing Young Black and White men and Criminal Records*, Ann Am Acad Pol Soc Sci, May 2009, 623 (1), 195–213, *available at* http//www.ncbi.nih.gov/pmc/article/PMC3583356.

DOI: 10.1057/9781137408433.0006

75   *See, EEOC v. Peoplemark, Inc.,* 732 F. 3d 584 (6th Cir.) (2012) (EEOC required
     to pay expert fees of employer where it was determined the employer did not
     have a broad no-hire policy for ex-felons).

76   *See,* Allan G. King & Rod M. Fliegel, *Conviction Records and Disparate Impact,*
     26 ABA *J. of Lab. & Employ.* L 405 426 (2011),

77   Jamie Fellner & Marc Mauer, the Sentencing Project Losing the Vote: *The Impact
     of Felony Disenfranchisement Laws in the United States, Human Rights Watch*
     (October 1998), *available at www.sentencingproject.org/doc/…/fd_losingthevote.
     pdf.*

78   Christopher Uggen, Sarah Shannon, & Jeff Manza, *State-Level Estimates
     of Felon Disenfranchisement in the United States, 2010, the Sentencing Project*
     (JULY 2012), [Hereinafter *Sentencing Project*], *available at* http://www.
     sentencingproject.org/detail/news.cfm?news_id=1334.

79   Marla Mcdaniel et al., *Imprisonment and Disenfranchisement of Disconnected
     Low-income Men. U.S. Department of Health & Human Services, Urban
     Institute* (August 2013), *available at* http://www.prisonpolicy.org/research/
     felon_disenfranchisement/.

80   *U.S.: Florida Ex-Offenders Barred from Vote, 31% of States African American Men
     Denied Vote, Human Rights Watch* (August 11, 2000), *available at* http://hrw.
     org/english/docs/2000/11/08/usclom603.htm (last visited May 28, 2014).

81   2013 U.S. Dist. LEXIS 40461,, 2013 WL 1193357 (March 22, 2013).

82   *Baker v. Pataki,* 85 F.3d 9/9 (2d Cir. 1996); *Farvakham v. Locke,* 987 F. Supp.
     1304 (E.D. Wash. 1997); *Johnson v. Governor of Florida,* 405 F. 3d 1214 (11th Cir.
     2005).

83   418 U.S. 24 (1974); *Wesley* 605 F.Supp. 802 (M.D. Tenn. 1985), *aff'd,* 791 F.2d
     1255 (6th Cir. 1986).

84   42 U.S.C. §1973; Andrew Shapiro, *Challenging Criminal Disenfranchisement
     under the Voting Rights Act: A New Strategy,* 103 Yale. L. Rev. 537–566 (1993).

85   *Wesley* at 802; *Farrakhan v. Gregoire,* 2006 U.S. Dist. LEXIS 45987, July 7, 2006;
     Muntagim v. Coombe, 366 F. 3d 102 (2nd Cir. 2004).

86   Civil Actions No. CV_2005_5778_RSV (2006), For a history of appeals
     and related cases, *see The Brenan Center for Justice, available at* http://www.
     brennancenter.org/legal-work/gooden-v-worley (last visited May 28, 2014).

87   2006 U.S. DIST. LEXIS 45987 July 7, 2006; Marc Mauser, *Ex-felons Denied
     Basic Right to Vote, Seattle Post, available at* http://seattlepi.nw.source.
     com/277513_sentencing14.html (last visited May 28, 2014).

88   2006 U.S. Dist. LEXIS 45987, July 7, 2006.

89   418 U.S. 24 (1974); Also, see, *U.S. v. Green,* 995 F.2d 793 (8th Cir. 1993).

90   But *see, Hunter v. Underwood,* 471 U.S. 222 (1985) (the Court held that
     Alabama disenfranchisement statute was unconstitutional under the Equal
     Protection Clause, because it was passed to discriminate against African-
     Americans).

DOI: 10.1057/9781137408433.0006

91   *Richardson v. Ramirez* 418 U.S. 24, 79 (197).

92   *See, Sentencing Project, Felony Disenfranchisement: A Primer* (update April 2014), *available at* http://sentencingproject.org/detail/publication. cfm?publication_id=502 (last visited May 28, 2014).

93   *See*, Section II (A) Mass Incarceration of African-American Males.

94   *See*, Ryan S. King & Marc Mauer, *The Sentencing Project the Vanishing Black Electorate: Felony Disenfranchisement in Atlanta, Georgia* (September 2004), *available at* http://www.sentencingproject.org/detail/publication. cfm?publication_id=23 (last visited May 28, 2014); Also *see* Lerone Bennett Jr., *Before the Mayflower a History of Black America*, 1969 4th ed, pp. 216–219 (Describes how Southern states disenfranchised African-Americans from voting).

95   *Sentencing Project. Democracy Imprisoned: A Review of the provence and Impact of Felony Disenfranchisement Laws in the United States* (September 2013), *available at* http://sentencingproject.org/doc/publications/fd_ICCPR%20 Felony%20Disenfranchisement%20Shadow%20Report (lasted visited May 28, 2014) (Because states are rapidly changing their disenfranchisement laws, all numbers cited in this section should be updated before citing.): Sentencing Project, Current Impact of Disenfranchisement Laws, *available at* http://www.sentencing project; cf. Darryl Fears, *In Atlanta 14% of Black Men Can't Vote. Washington Post,* Thursday September 23, 2004, p. A-10.

96   *See, Sentencing Project, supra* note 2.

97   *See id.*

98   *See id.*

99   *See id.*

100   *See id.*; Also see, Mississippi State Chapter, *Operation PUSH v. Allain,* 674 F. Supp. 1245, 1251–1252 (N.D. Miss. 1987) (discusses the history of voting rights discrimination in the state of Mississippi).

101   133 S. Ct. 2612 (2013).

102   *See Hethering v. State Personnel Board,* 82 Cal. App. 3d 582 (1978) (African-American males challenge State law prohibiting employment of ex-felon as state Peace Officers).

103   Devah Pager, *The Mark of a Criminal Record,* 108 *Am. J. Soc.* 937 (2003).

104   U.S. Dep't of Justice, *Federal Statutes Imposing Collateral Consequences upon Conviction, available at* http://www.usdoj.gov/par./on/Col.; Jerome G. Miller, Unanticipated Consequences of the Justice System, *In Search And Destroy, African-American Males In The Criminal Justice System,* 1996, pp. 89–136.

105   Adam Goldman, *Eric Holder Makes Case For Felons To Get Voting Rights Back, Washington Post,* February 11, 2014, *available at* http://www.washingtonpost. com/world/national-security/eric-holder-.

106   Christopher Uggen, *Barriers to Democratic Participation, Prisoner Reentry and the Institution of Civil Society: Bridges and Barriers to Successful*

DOI: 10.1057/9781137408433.0006

Reintegration (March 2002) (unnumbered working paper), *available at* www. urbaninstitute.org/UploadedPDF/410801_Barriers.pdf (discusses "the scope and likely political impact of disenfranchisement on state and national elections").

107 *See generally,* Geneva Brown, *White Man's Justice, Black Man's Grief: Voting Disenfranchisement and the Failure of the Social Contract,* 110 *Berkeley J. Afr. Am. L. & Pol'y* 287 (2008); Dhami Mandeepk, Prisoner Dienfranchisement Policy: A Threat to Democracy? *Analyses of Soc. Iss. & Pub Pol'y,* 235 (2005).

108 Erika Harrell, *U.S. Dep't of Justice, Bureau of Justice Stat., Black Victims of Violent Crime* (August, 2007), *available at* http://www.bjs.gov/content/pub/pdf/bvvc.pdf.

109 *Id.*; Jeffrey A. Roth, *U.S. Justice Dep't, National Inst. of Justice, Understanding and Preventing Violence* 2 (February 1994), *available at* cagisperm. hamilton-co.org/cpop/documents/library/Understanding%20....

110 Erica l. Smith & Alexia Cooper, *U.S. Department of Justice, Office of Justice Statistic, Homicide Trends in the Unites States, 1980–2008 Annual Rates for 2009 and 2010* (November 2011), *available at* http://www.bis.gov/content/pub/ascii/htus8oo8.txt.

111 Erica l. Smith & Alexia Cooper, *U.S. Dep't of Justice, Bureau of Justice Statistics, Homicide in the U.S. Known to Law Enforcement,* 2011 (December 2013), *available at* http://www.bjs.gov/index.cfm?ty=pbdetail&iid=4863.

112 *Id.* at 9.

113 Arline T. Geronimus et al., *Excess Mortality Among Blacks and Whites in the United States,* 335 *New Eng. J. Med.* 1552 (1996), *available at* www.nejm.org.

114 *U.S. Dep't of Health and Human Serv., Centers for Disease Control & Prevention, National Center for Health Stat.* (January 6, 2014), *available at* http://www.cdc.gov/nchs/nvss/mortality/lewk3.htm.

115 S. Jay Olshansky et al., *Differences in Life Expectancy Due to race and Educational Differences Are Widening, And Many May Not Catch Up,* 31 *Health Affairs* 1803 (August 2012), *available at* healthaffairs.org/content/31/8/1803.

116 *American Cancer Society, Cancer Facts & Figures for African Americans, 2011–2012* (2011), *available at* www.cancer.org/acs/.../acspc-027765.

117 *U.S. Dep't of Health and Human Services, Centers for Disease Control and Prevention, Current Cigarette Smoking Adults Aged 18 and Over, by Sex, Race, and Age: United States, Selected Years* 1965–2012 (2012), *available at* http://www.cdc.gov/nchs/hus/contents2012.htm#054.

118 *American Lung Association, African American and Lung Cancer* (April 10, 2010), *available at* http://www.lung.org/about-us/our-impact/top-stories/african-americans-and-lung-cancer.html.

119 *Centers for Disease Control and Prevention, Lung Cancer in African-American Men* (September 25, 2013), *available at* http://www.cdc.gov/cancer/lung/basic_info/infographic.htm.

DOI: 10.1057/9781137408433.0006

120   Am. *Cancer Soc'y, Cancer Facts & Figures for African Americans* 9 (2011–2012), *available at* www.cancer.org/acs/ . . . /acspc-027765.

121   *Centers for Disease Control and Prevention, African American/Blacks, Hiv/ Aids* (2012), *available at* http://www.cdc.gov/nchhstp/healthdisparities/ AfricanAmericans.html.

122   *Id.*

123   *See,* Lloyd Gite, *Black Men and Suicide,* ESSENCE (November 1986) (reporting on how racism leads to depression and low self-esteem which can ultimately lead to suicide by African-American males); Also see, Robert C. Evans & Helen Evans, *Coping: Stressors and Depression Among Middle Class African American Men,* 1 *J. African Am. Men* 29 (Fall 1995).

124   *U.S. Census, Income, Poverty and Health Insurance Coverage in the United States: 2012* (September 17, 2013), *available at* http://www.census.gov/newsroom/ releases/archives/poverty/.

125   *See,* Eric M. Bridges, *Racial Identity Development and Psychological Coping Strategies of Undergraduate and Graduate African-American Males,* 2 *J. African Am. Males in Ed.* 150 (Summer 2011). *available at* http:// journalofafricanamericanmales.com/wp-content/plugins/download-monitor/download.php?id=38.

126   David H. Chae, Amani M. Nuru-Jeter, Nancy E. Adler, Jue Lin, Elizabeth H. Blackburn, Elissa S. Epel and Gene H. Brody, *Discrimination, Racial Bias. And Telomere Length in African-American Men,* 46 *Am. J. Med.* 103 (January 7, 2014), *available at* www.ncbi.nlm.nih.gov/; Tony N. Brown, David R. Williams, James S. Jackson, Harold W. Neighbors, Myriam Torres, Sherrill L. Sellers and Kendrick T. Brown, *Being Black and Feeling Blue: The Mental Health Consequences of Racial Discrimination,* 2 RACE & SOC'Y 131, *available at* http://www.researchgate.net/publication/223532749_Being_black_and_ feeling_blue_the_mental_health_consequences_of_racial_discrimination/ file/79e4150c0a58e20eba.pdf.

127   Debra Umberson, Kristi Williams, Patricia A. Thomas, Hui Liu and Mieke Beth Thomeer, *Race, Gender, and Chains of Disadvantage: Childhood Adversity, Social Relationships, and Health,* 55 *J. Health and Social Behavior,* 20 (2014), *available at* http://www.asanet.org/journals/JHSB/MAR14JHSBFeature.pdf.

128   *U.S. Department of Health and Human Services, Agency for Healthcare Research and Quality, 2012 National Healthcare Disparities Report* (May 2013), *available at* http://www.ahrq.gov/research/findings/nhqrdr/nhdr12/.

129   David E. Newman Toker, Ernest Moy, Ernest Valente, Rosanna Coffey and Anika L. Hines, *Missed Diagnosis of Stroke in the Emergency Department: A Cross-Sectional Analysis of a Large Population-Based Sample* (2014), *available at* www.degruyter.com/view/j/ . . . /dx-2013-0038.xml? (last visited May 28, 2014).

130   Laura Schmidt, Thomas Greenfield and Nina Mulia, *National Institute on Alcoholism Unequal Treatment, Racial and Ethnic Disparities in Alcoholism*

DOI: 10.1057/9781137408433.0006

Treatment Services (2006), *available at* http://pubs.niaaa.nih.gov/
publications/arh291/49-54.htm.

131   *The National Institute on Drug Abuse, Nih Health Disparities Strategic Plan,
Fiscal Years 2009–2013, available at* http://www.nei.nih.gov/strategicplanning/
disparities_strategic_plan.asp.

132   *See*, Vernellia R. Randall, *Inequality in Health is Killing Africans Americans*, 36,
20 (2009); Brain D. Smedley, Adrienne Y. Stith and Alan R. Nelson, *Unequal
Treatment: Confronting Racial and Ethnic Disparities in Health Care*, 2003,
available at Http://Www.Nap.Edu/Catalog/10260.Html; Gillian K. Fisher,
*The Commonwealth Fund, Addressing Unequal Treatment; Disparities in Health
Care, Issue Brief* (November 2004), *available at* www.commonwealthfund.
org.

DOI: 10.1057/9781137408433.0006

4
Conclusion

Abstract: *This chapter finds that the plight of African-American males is clearly a tragedy. It is a tragedy that repeats itself over and over in every American institution system. An overwhelming number of empirical studies and reports conclude that disparity in the treatment of African-American males exists in the justice system. Similarly, other institutional systems mirror the same negative disparities between African-American males and nonminorities.*

Weatherspoon, Floyd. *African-American Males and the U.S. Justice System of Marginalization: A National Tragedy.* New York: Palgrave Macmillan, 2014. DOI: 10.1057/9781137408433.0007.

DOI: 10.1057/9781137408433.0007

The plight of African-American males is clearly a tragedy. It is a tragedy that repeats itself over and over in every American institutional system. An overwhelming number of empirical studies and reports conclude that disparity in the treatment of African-American males exists in the justice system. Similarly, other institutional systems mirror the same negative disparities between African-American males and nonminorities. Even institutional policies and practices that appear to be neutral on their face have a disparate impact on minorities, African-American males in particular. This disparity is the result of stereotypical biases and racism intentionally and unintentionally directed at African-American males. Many African-American males appear to have fallen prey to negative stereotypical biases which permeate throughout the justice and other institutional systems.

As a result of the disparities, stereotypical biases, and racism in the justice and institutional systems, the status of many African-American males has reached a crisis. Ironically, the courts and Congress have repeatedly acknowledged the disparities, even racism, within the various systems, but nevertheless have failed to issue or promulgate corrective action. Instead, the criminal justice system continues to disproportionately "lock them up." Congress and state legislatures continue to propose additional legislation to lock up even more, and law enforcement agencies target African-American males for arrest and prosecution. Clearly, racism and disparity also exist in the civil justice system. African-American males have little faith that they will receive equal justice, particularly in a system where judges are biased, where there is a lack of adequate legal representation for minorities, and where minorities are disproportionately underrepresented in the justice system work force.

DOI: 10.1057/9781137408433.0007

Index

DOI: 10.1057/9781137408433.0008

incarceration—*Continued*
Washington 20
West Virginia 25
white males 21, 24
Wisconsin 20
Individual with Disabilities Act
(IDEA) *see* education

Jena Six 3
juvenile justice system 56–59
Action for Children 58
Cook County, IL 58
disproportionality 57
Florida 56–57
harsher sentencing 20, 58
Law School Admissions
Council
Meridian, MS 58–59
National Council on Crime &
Delinquency 58
school-to-prison pipeline 58
war on drugs 56

movies 13
Boyz N the Hood 13
Baby Boy 13
Driving Miss Daisy 13
Glover, Danny 14
New Jack City 13
Juice 13
Perry, Tyler 13
The Butler 13
Training Day 13
Twelve Years a Slave 13
Waiting to Exhale 13

Pew Charitable Trust 19
police brutality 50–52
Byrd, James 5
Chicago 51
Columbus, OH 51
Denver 51
Diallo, Amadou 5, 51
Ferrell, Jonathan 5
Green, Malice 5, 51
King, Rodney 5, 50

Los Angeles 50
Morgan, Joe 51
New York 50–51
Oakland 50
President Obama 5–6, 9, 15
prisons 19–26
Angola Prison 23–24
California 24
correctionalofficers 25
correctional population 4, 19
drug laws 24
farm 24
federal prisons 23
New Orleans 23
parole 3, 25
prisoners 3, 25
prison for profit 25
probation 3, 25
racial disparities 23
state prisons 23
Violent Crime Control Act 24
warehousing 19
prosecutorial decisions 48
Florida 49
McCleskey v. Kemp 49
plea bargaining 48
racial disparities 48
Vera's Prosecution and Racial
District Program 49

racial profiling 26–44
abuse 17–18
airport stops 38–39
Arizona 33
Black America's Political Action
Committee 28
black males 26
buses 39
City of Torrance 29
defined 27
Dred Scott v. Sanford 38
"driving while black" 30
drug courier profile 39, 40
Drug Enforcement Agency (DEA)
39–40
economic status 28

DOI: 10.1057/9781137408433.0008

DOI: 10.1057/9781137408433.0008

CPSIA information can be obtained at www.ICGtesting.com
Printed in the USA
LVOW11*2043300115

425057LV00005B/33/P